Xbox Fan Book

Rock the BoX

by Mark Holt Walker

Copyright © 2005 O'Reilly Media, Inc.
Printed in the United States of America.
Published by O'Reilly Media, Inc.
1005 Gravenstein Highway North, Sebastopol, CA 95472.

O'Reilly books may be purchased for educational, business, or sales promotional use. Online editions are also available for most titles (*safari.oreilly.com*). For more information, contact our corporate/institutional sales department: 800-998-9938 or *corporate@oreilly.com*.

Xbox Fan Book
Rock the BoX
by Mark Holt Walker

Print History

November 2004: First Edition.

Editor:
Brian Jepson

Photographer:
Mark Holt Walker

Production Editor:
Darren Kelly

Art Director:
Michele Wetherbee

Cover Designer:
Ellie Volckhausen

Interior Designer:
Aufuldish & Warinner
www.aufwar.com

Illustrators:
Robert Romano
Jessamyn Read

Copyeditor:
Nancy Reinhardt

Indexer:
Julie Hawks

ISBN: 0-596-00884-8

[W]

Contents

Preface

✖ xʙox

The Xbox Fan Book

Welcome to the console revolution. Game consoles have existed for nearly four decades, but it was not until the distribution of what are commonly called *second generation consoles* (consoles that use 128-bit memory streams) that the video game business began to boom. These debuted with the release of Sega's Dreamcast, which is no longer produced, in 1999 (December 1998 in Japan), followed by Sony's PlayStation 2 in 2000, and Nintendo's Gamecube and Microsoft's Xbox in 2001.

Of the four second-generation consoles, the Xbox boasts the most powerful processor and graphics chip, and is the only one of the four to include a hard drive within the console. Gamers have snatched them up at an amazing rate. As of September 2004, almost 15 million were in gamers' hands, and the demand hasn't slowed. In fact, sales of Xbox consoles and peripherals (aftermarket controllers and such) have increased over 12 percent in 2004, compared to the previous years' sales.

It is that enthusiasm for the Xbox and its games that prompted the writing of the *Xbox Fan Book*. There are millions of Xbox gamers spread across the globe, and all of them want to know how to get the most out of their Xbox without spending a lot of time searching numerous books.

The machine in the box

Microsoft's Xbox has been called a computer without a keyboard, and in fact, hackers have morphed it into just that—a powerful computer capable of running Linux and performing most, if not all, of what users have come to expect from a desktop computer. Hacking the Xbox, however, is beyond the scope of this book. If you are interesting in extensively hacking the Xbox, I suggest reading *Hacking the Xbox: An Introduction to Reverse Engineering* by Andrew Huang (No Starch Press). The point is that the machine inside the box is a very capable computer, one that is complete with a hard drive and semi-cutting-edge graphics card, and that delivers the *best* performance of any console on the market.

The Microsoft Xbox

Preface

Up and
Running

Maximizing
Your Xbox
Experience

Networking
the Xbox

Take it
Online with
Xbox Live

Xbox
Accessories

Xbox
Buyer's Guide

The Future
Is Bright

X xbox

x

The Xbox hardware

Hands down, Microsoft's Xbox is the most capable of the second-generation consoles, but exactly how capable is it? The following table displays its capabilities and the capabilities of its nearest rivals, Nintendo's GameCube and Sony's PlayStation 2.

	Microsoft Xbox	PlayStation 2	GameCube
Processor	733 MHz	294 MHz	485MHz
Memory (RAM)	64MB	32MB	43MB
Graphics Processor	NVidia GPU 256-bit graphics 2D/3D	Emotion GPU 128-bit Graphics 2D/3D	ATI GPU 64-bit Graphics 2D/3D
Hard Drive	Yes	Yes (with add-on)	No
Internet Capable	Yes	Yes (with adapter)	Yes (with adapter)
DVD Playback	Yes (with adapter)	Yes	No

Processor

The processor is a good yardstick for a computer's overall speed. When the Xbox was introduced in 2001, 733 MHz was *fast*. Now there are computers on the market with speeds of over 3 GHz! That doesn't, however, tell the complete tale. Although computers are much faster than consoles, PC game programmers must code their software to work on multiple types of computers. Xbox programmers need only optimize their code to work on one machine. Hence Xbox games still produce visuals and frame rates (the speed at which the video card refreshes the picture) that make them competitive with the latest PC games.

Memory (RAM)

Random Access Memory or RAM is the memory the computer uses to run programs. Think of it as short-term memory, where the processor stores the information it needs. The more RAM a computer has, the faster—everything else being equal—the computer will run. Microsoft's Xbox has more RAM than any other console, and it shows in the speed of the Xbox.

Graphics processor

All three consoles are capable of running 3D (three-dimensional graphics), but the Xbox runs them more quickly and with greater clarity. Notice that the table compares the "bits" that each processor can process. This is analogous to the size of a pipe; the bigger the pipe, the greater the amount of liquid that it can deliver in the same amount of time. Staying with this analogy, Xbox's 256-bit processor is the widest pipe, and it delivers the most realistic, lush, and fastest graphics.

Hard drive

Desktop and laptop users will be intimately familiar with this (the thing that's never big enough to hold everything you need). The hard drive is where computers store long-term information such as files and installed programs. The Xbox is the only console that has a hard drive. If you wish to save games on the Gamecube or PlayStation you must first buy a memory card that inserts into the front of the machine. No such extra is needed with the Xbox. The Xbox hard drive may be used to save games and for other purposes that I cover later in the book. Not only is the Xbox's hard drive convenient, but saving and accessing files on the hard drive is quicker than using a memory card.

> The PlayStation 2 also supports an add-on internal hard drive, which is included with both *Final Fantasy XI* and the *Linux (for PlayStation 2) Kit*. However, not all PlayStation 2 games will save to the hard drive.

Internet capable

The Xbox is Internet-ready. To hook up to Xbox Live you need only plug in a broadband or LAN connection to the Xbox, and you are off to the races (you can also connect the Xbox to a WiFi network). I go into this in more detail in Chapters 3 and 4.

DVD playback

Of the four second-generation consoles, only the PlayStation 2 ships ready to play DVDs. To play them on Microsoft's Xbox, you need to buy the Xbox DVD playback kit. I discuss the playback kit in greater detail in Chapter 5, but its installation is simple, and the investment (less than thirty dollars) is much less expensive than buying a separate DVD player. The playback kit also includes a remote, so you won't need to control your movie with the game pad the way you must with a PlayStation 2. Playback kits bought in the U.S., its territories, and Canada allow you to play DVDs from that region (Region 1) only. The Xbox can be modified to play DVDs from all regions, and I address that in Chapter 5.

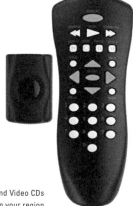

The DVD Playback Kit spins DVDs and Video CDs
(VCD) from your region

Xbox web resources

The more you know, the more you enjoy. Xbox enthusiasts won't be satisfied with popping the occasional game into their machine, they'll want more. They'll want to know what the hottest games are to pop in their machine, what accessories to hook up to it, and where to buy them. I can't tell you everything—well, actually I could, but then the printing prices would be astronomical. So I thought I'd throw out some of the best web sites that you can surf to glean the information that you need. So, in no intelligently discernable order, here are some sites that you might want to check out.

www.xbox.com

> The official Xbox site. Has a wealth of information on Xbox Live, some gaming accessories, and some semi-slanted (after all this *is* Microsoft's site) reviews.

www.xboxreporter.com

> One of the most inclusive sites on the Web. Includes everything from reviews, to news, to hardware updates, to practically everything. Includes lots of information on Xbox mod chips.

www.thenextbox.com

> This is *the* place to go to find out about the next generation Xbox. Excellent stuff on the future of the Box, and also information on the other next-generation consoles. Make sure you check out their forums.

www.xboxsolution.com

> Lots of news, not all of it official. Active, vociferous forums. Xbox-related wallpapers, and a huge cheat section.

www.xbox2news.com

> As the name indicates, this site is dedicated to news about the upcoming next-generation Xbox.

www.talkxbox.com

> This can't be a real Xbox site! It's not colored green and black. Nevertheless, there are reviews, screen shots, and tons more on this very informative site. Very well-rounded.

www.gamespot.com

> Gamespot is one of the—if not *the*—largest gaming portals on the Internet. The site includes everything from interviews and reviews, to strategy guides and cheats. Extensive news section. This is the one stop for your gaming information fix.

www.ign.com

> Another massive Internet portal with a lot of information on the Xbox. Similar to Gamespot.

Xbox magazines

All the gaming magazines have similar content; most come with a DVD that holds playable game demos. There are two major magazines, both of which are monthly: *The Official Xbox Magazine* and *Xbox Nation Magazine (XBN)*.

01

Up and Running

The Xbox close up

The Xbox is a simple machine, and that's exactly the way Microsoft wanted it. Viewed from the top, you see a plain box approximately 12 by 10 by 3 inches. There is no deep insight to share about the top of the box, just don't step on it, hit it with heavy blunt instruments, or fire armor-piercing weapons in its direction.

The Xbox from above

X xbox

Ah, now the front view of the Xbox is a little more complex. Again, please do not hit it with hammers or projectiles. The four ports are for controllers, the DVD adapter, or other accessories. Remember to insert the controller (or DVD adapter) plug notched side up. This position ensures that the contacts mate correctly with the contacts inside the Xbox. The small center button is the power switch, and the larger button opens and closes the DVD tray.

The front view of the Xbox

X xbox

4

The rear of the Xbox has three ports. From left to right, they are the power jack, audio/video (AV) jack, and Ethernet port. Plug the power cord into the power jack, and your AV cable into the AV jack. The Ethernet port is where your broadband cable or system cable snaps in. Oh yeah, don't step on this side either.

The rear view of the Xbox showing its ports

Hook up your Xbox

Now that you understand your Xbox's capabilities, it's time to hook it up and dive right in. Doing this is really quite simple. Remove the Xbox and the cables from the carton. Included with each Xbox are the following:

- The Xbox.

- The controller and connecting cable.

- The audio-video (AV) cable. This is the cable that splits into three colored wires (yellow, red, and white) at one end, and a broad connector on the other.

- The power cable.

- The instruction booklet.

The controller: this is where the gaming begins

Preface

Up and
Running

Maximizing
Your Xbox
Experience

Networking
the Xbox

Take it
Online with
Xbox Live

Xbox
Accessories

Xbox
Buyer's Guide

The Future
Is Bright

X XBOX

6

The AV cable; if there's nothing in your box that looks like this, you're in trouble!

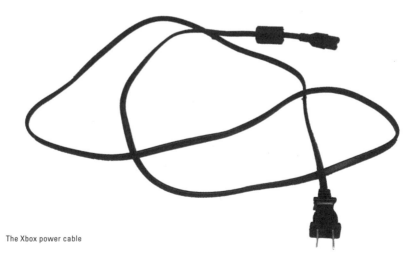

The Xbox power cable

Find a good home for your Xbox

Remember, the Xbox is a computer, and computers need to stay cool. This particular computer also needs to stay flat. So, to make a semi-long story short, you should place the Xbox in a well-ventilated area that has room for the Xbox to rest horizontally.

Ventilation openings line the side and rear of the Xbox; they look like louvers. Blocking these openings will cause the Xbox to overheat, and although their location and purpose may seem obvious, it only takes a small bit of inattention to block the openings. For example, stuffing the Xbox into an entertainment center cubby that it "fits perfectly" will most likely restrict the flow of air to the ventilation openings. In a similar manner, plopping the Xbox on a couch will also cause it to overheat when the cushions on either side of it block the ventilation openings.

A lightweight television may be placed on top of the Xbox (no ventilation openings there), and the Xbox may be placed on other electronic equipment, but make sure the equipment does not force hot air into the Xbox's ventilation openings. To avoid extension cords, place the machine close to both an electrical outlet and the television to which you wish to hook it up.

Close-up of the Xbox ventilation openings. Keep these open and free of dust bunnies if you want to keep your Xbox cool.

Hook up the AV cable to a television

Ensure that your Xbox is unplugged, just to be on the safe side. There's no need risking your Xbox to stray electrical currents. Next, plug the AV cable into its port on the center back of your Xbox and then push the color coded connectors in to the corresponding jacks on the television. Non-stereo televisions will only have one audio jack. In such cases, you can plug either the left or right audio connector to it. If you have an older TV that does not have the appropriate jacks you'll need to buy an adapter kit from www.xbox.com or another suitable web site or store. You may also plug the connector cables into a VCR that routes AV signals to your TV.

Connect the AV cable to the Xbox

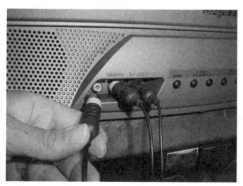

Connect the AV cable to your TV or home theater system

Play a game!

Plug in the controller, select video input on your television, and you are ready to play. Discovering how to enable video input on your TV is not always easy. If your television or remote has a Game setting or a TV/Video option, select it. That will usually do the trick. If not, select AUX or Source. If you're using an RF adapter for an older TV, or if you're routing AV through a VCR, selecting a low channel, such as 3 or 4, will usually work, and on very rare occasions, a higher channel might work.

Plug the controller into the Xbox

Finding your way around

If you start the Xbox with a game in the DVD drive you'll immediately be taken to the game's main menu. If you start the Xbox *without* a game in the DVD drive, the Xbox main menu will pop onto your television screen. From this screen, you may set the Xbox to suit your preferences. There are four options that you may access from the main Xbox menu. They are:

- Memory
- Music
- Xbox Live
- Settings

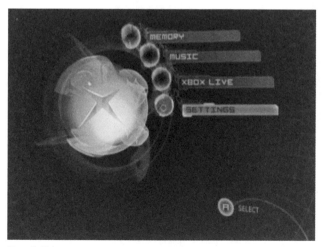

The main Xbox menu

Memory

Highlight Memory and press the A button to access the Xbox memory. From the memory you may look at what files you have stored on the console's hard drive. The Xbox comes with eight gigabytes of hard drive space, divided into 50,000+ blocks of memory. Each game save uses some of these blocks of memory. If you ever fill the hard drive—an unlikely occurrence—you can delete saved games. Press the A button to access the hard drive, flick through the saved games with the D-Pad, and delete the selected file/saved game by once again pressing the A button.

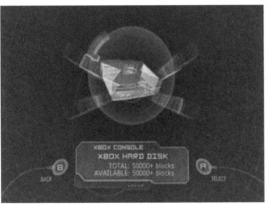

Viewing the Xbox memory

Music

Select Music to play a CD, or copy music from a CD already inserted into the CD/DVD tray. To play a new CD, slip it into the tray, slide the tray into the machine, and the play menu appears. Some artists slap a video or two on their CDs. The Xbox will not play these videos, nor any other VCD (video CD), without an installed DVD playback kit.

On the other hand, computers will most often detect VCD elements and play them. If they don't however, you can usually play a VCD by opening Windows Explorer, browsing to the MPEGAV folder on the VCD, opening it, and then clicking on the DAT file. Associate it with your media player, and away you go.

The Xbox can also copy songs from your favorite CD. Heck, it will even copy music from CDs that you don't like, but why would you want to do that? Choose Copy from the music menu. Select the tracks that you want to copy, and then select the playback list—or make a new one—that you want to copy them to. After you create a playback list you may access and play it from the Music menu. If your musical tastes change, you may also remove the songs, which frees up hard drive space.

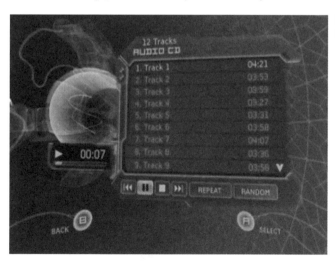

Play music on your Xbox

Preface

Up and
Running

Maximizing
Your Xbox
Experience

Networking
the Xbox

Take it
Online with
Xbox Live

Xbox
Accessories

Xbox
Buyer's Guide

The Future
Is Bright

X XBOX

14

Xbox Live

On Xbox Live you can meet friends, make friends, and then kick their tails in some of the best online gaming in the world. I cover it all in Chapter 4. Don't miss it.

Settings

From the Settings menu you may change how your Xbox is configured in a variety of way. Most of these changes are covered in greater detail in Chapters 2, 3, and 4, so I will just briefly explain their purpose here.

Clock

Set your clock and time zone from this menu.

Language

Choose one from Xbox's nine languages here.

Audio

Choose the audio that matches your television sound set–up. The options are: Mono (for TVs without stereo sound), Stereo, and Dolby Surround (state of the art for the lucky folks).

Video

Select the video settings that match your TV. I explain these and how to maximize them in Chapter 2.

Network Settings

The Xbox is LAN capable. This menu provides access to the LAN settings. I cover this in nearly nauseating detail in Chapter 3.

Auto Sign-In

Here you can choose to automatically sign in to Xbox Live with your last used sign-in. In other words, if you are the only person using the Xbox, you'll have your Live username and password ready to go whenever you sign in.

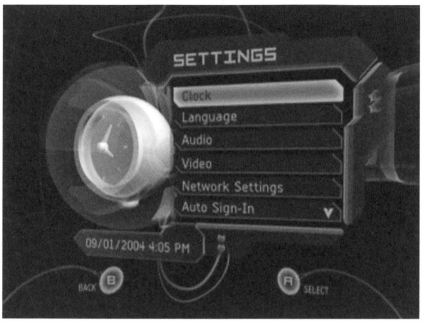

The Xbox settings screen

Parental Control

The Parental Control menu allows users to set the limits on the games and DVDs viewed on their Xbox. Consult Chapter 2 for additional information.

Auto Off

A simple, yet cool, feature. Enabling Auto Off automatically shuts down the Xbox if it has been idle for six hours. All night gaming sessions aside, it's not a good idea to run the Xbox longer than need be. This feature ensures that your console doesn't run when you don't need it. On the flip side of the disk, sometimes you'll want the Xbox to run. If you are in the middle of a level without a *save point*, and don't want to lose your progress, the only alternative is to let the game run while you're at work. Unless, like me, your work *is* playing games, but then you have other creatures (a significant other, children, pets, the undead, giant robots, etc.) to contend with, and that's another book.

If you're primarily a computer gamer, you may be used to games where you can save at any time. Some console games use *save points* instead, special places in a game where you can save your game. It may be a location you must return to or simply a Save Game option that's offered between levels. Not all games rely on save points, but you'll probably run into some that do.

System Info

Boring copyright stuff.

Your Xbox controller

Microsoft has put a lot of thought into the controller, so let's take a few minutes to look at it and understand how to best employ it. You'll find that the time spent here will pay big dividends later.

Joysticks

There are two thumb joysticks on your controller. They are often used to control your direction of movement in racing games or first-person shooters, and to scroll through menus. In some games, such as *MechAssault*, the left stick controls movement and the right controls where you look. Hence, you may look in one direction while moving in another. Please, don't try to do that in the real world.

Directional Pad

Between the two joysticks is the *Directional Pad* or *D-Pad*. The D-Pad is used for a similar function as the joysticks. There is, however, a significant difference. The D-Pad is basically an off-on switch. Press a direction and your car, BattleMech, marine, or whatever will move that way. The D-Pad doesn't control how fast he is moving; he either is or he isn't. The Joysticks usually control the "amount" of input, and hence how fast your car, BattleMech, or marine moves.

Start/Back Buttons

To the left of the D-Pad are the Start/Back buttons. They are game and menu specific, but usually perform actions synonymous with their names. The Start button begins a game or level, the Back button returns you to the previous menu screen.

White/Black Buttons

These buttons perform game-specific functions and are not used on the generic Xbox menus.

A Button

Usually pressed to select an action. Think of this button as the "yes" button. It may also fire weapons in some games, or accelerate a vehicle. The A button always means "select" on the generic Xbox menus and Dashboard.

X Button

Game-specific button.

Y Button

Game-specific button.

B Button

Usually pressed to return to the previous menu, or to de-select an option in a game. B always means "back" on the generic Xbox menus and Dashboard.

Left and Right Triggers

The triggers are located on the front of the controller. They are used for a variety of functions. In *Full Spectrum Warrior*, they can select individual soldiers. In *MechAssault* they cycle through the various weapons. These triggers can also be used to fire weapons, and in some racing games like *Rallisport Challenge* the triggers control acceleration and brakes.

The Xbox controller, close-up

X Y

Joystick

Back

Start

B

A

Black

White

Directional pad

The Xbox controller from above

Right trigger

Left trigger

Preface

Up and
Running

Maximizing
Your Xbox
Experience

Networking
the Xbox

Take it
Online with
Xbox Live

Xbox
Accessories

Xbox
Buyer's Guide

The Future
Is Bright

X xbox

20

That first game

Okay, you're ready. Pop that first game into the Xbox, sit back on the couch with your favorite beverage, a bag of Tostitos, and some cheese dip (the hot kind), and you're ready to start playing.

Press the eject button to open the tray, carefully put the game DVD in the tray, and press the eject button again to close the tray

02

Maximizing Your Xbox Experience

If this book weren't part of the *Fan Book* series, this chapter's title would probably be the book's title. In a nutshell, maximizing your Xbox experience is what I am trying to do. This chapter, however, specifically covers the audio, visual, and even ergonomic tweaks that you can make to maximize how your Xbox looks, sounds, and plays.

Here, I cover some basic techniques and equipment that enhance the Xbox's already excellent graphics, tell you how you can get the most from your game's sound, and show you how to set up your living room, gaming room, or den to maximize your Xbox experience. Finally I throw down some basic techniques to up your gaming game. After all, if you can't beat what you are playing, all the audio and video enhancing in the world won't make a console fun. These techniques won't necessarily put you at the top of the *MechAssault* Xbox Live ladder; it would take more pages, tips, and practice to accomplish that. But I'll discuss some basic techniques newbie Xbox gamers should learn right upfront.

Enhancing Xbox graphics

Xbox visuals are great right out of the box. There are, however, add-ons to improve them.

Xbox High Definition AV Pack

With the addition of the High Definition AV pack (about $20) you can play your Xbox games in all the glory of High Definition TV (HDTV). This pack feeds the Xbox input into televisions with interlaced component video inputs that are capable of displaying 480i and either 720p or 1080i component video signals.

The High Definition AV pack

Preface

Up and
Running

Maximizing
Your Xbox
Experience

Networking
the Xbox

Take it
Online with
Xbox Live

Xbox
Accessories

Xbox
Buyer's Guide

The Future
Is Bright

X XBOX

22

Great, you say, but what does that mean? The typical North American TV displays its pictures—both games and DVD movies—in 525 lines; half the lines are refreshed every 60th of a second. This is called *interlacing*. However, only 485 lines are used for the actual image (40 lines contain encoded data such as closed captioning), and each line contains a continuous stream of colors; depending on the quality of the television and the type of input, that stream of colors compares to something between 220 and 540 dots (or *pixels*). This yields a maximum resolution of 540 x 485 (horizontal pixels by vertical pixels). Although it's much less than typical computer resolutions, television viewers are used to it, and it works fine.

Computer users, however, frequently run their monitors at resolutions of 1024 x 768. With HDTV, up to 1080i, or 1080 lines are projected, and that works out to 1920 x 1080 pixels.

Not only are there more pixels on the screen with HDTV, but the manner in which they are displayed is better. Remember the interlaced scan in normal TV? HDTV uses a different type of refresh method called *progressive scanning,* in which all of the lines—top to bottom—are refreshed simultaneously. Hence, there is no screen flicker, but there is one heck of a beautiful picture. So, if you have an HDTV, buying the High Definition AV pack is a *must*.

Preface

Up and
Running

Maximizing
Your Xbox
Experience

Networking
the Xbox

Take it
Online with
Xbox Live

Xbox
Accessories

Xbox
Buyer's Guide

The Future
Is Bright

X xbox

24

There are, however, a few things to remember. The standard AV cable that ships with the Xbox will *not* hook directly to an HDTV, so don't even try. You'll also need a specially marked Xbox game to see the difference in definition. Games that are HDTV capable are marked on the back under the system requirements. There's an "X" beside the HDTV rectangle, and it will state something like HDTV 480p (lower resolution than 1080i, but still not bad). Finally, if you are using the DVD adapter to watch a flick, you must still have a HDTV-enhanced movie to view it in all its high definition glory. Regular DVDs will still work, but they won't look as stunning.

Microsoft's *Knights of the Old Republic* is an HDTV game

Xbox Advanced AV Pack

Use the Microsoft Xbox Advanced AV pack to connect to televisions that support optical digital audio input for Dolby Digital playback (it also supports the standard RCA connectors for left and right audio). This pack uses S-Video for the video display. Normally video signals are split into three parts; black and white information, and two color signals, which is the method used by the standard AV cable that ships with the Xbox. S-Video, however, is different; it splits its signal into two parts: The black and white signal (one part) and all the color signals.

As you might expect, combining the two color signals results in a degradation of the color information. In the grand scheme of things, this is a fairly minor degradation, and you still get an exceptionally good picture from this signal, much better than what you would see using the standard AV cable.

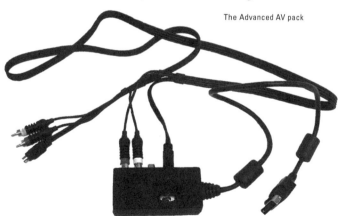

The Advanced AV pack

Two video connections; composite video is shown on the left, S-Video on the right

Optimizing the video environment

To a large extent, optimizing the visual environment is common sense. Never-theless, for those new to console gaming, here a few tips to keep in mind after you have set up your Xbox.

Ambient light

Get out in the sun every day. It's not only good for your soul but keeps you from getting that pasty white skin you see on so many of us gaming journalists. However, when you are gaming, it's best to play in a room with low light, and absolutely no glare on the TV screen. After all, how do you think we gaming journalists get that pasty white skin?

Distance

Hey, you don't want to get too far away from that TV screen. I mean closer is better, right? Wrong! I have it from a reliable source—i.e. my mother—that sitting too close to the screen will, in fact, suck your eyes out. Believe it or not there is a formula for this stuff, and here it is. You should sit no closer to your TV than twice the dimension of your screen. That said, it makes sense to give yourself at least 10 feet between the front of the television and your easy chair. It will improve your situational awareness and you'll have a better chance of catching action on the periphery of the screen.

The throne of games

Last, but by no stretch of the imagination least, you must have the proper chair to game properly. Soft, yet not slack, reclinable, but not horizontal, easy to get into, and just a tad hard to get out of (one more excuse to keep playing). Finally, it helps to have a friend, pet, or obedient robot with a flat head. Seat them beside you and place your favorite beverage on their noggin.

Preface

Up and Running

Maximizing Your Xbox Experience

Networking the Xbox

Take it Online with Xbox Live

Xbox Accessories

Xbox Buyer's Guide

The Future Is Bright

X xbox

26

The ESRB

The Entertainment Software Review Board, or ESRB (www.esrb.org) rating system is similar to movie ratings. It is a system that we can all rely on to describe the content within a game. The system has two parts: the actual rating, and the description or explanation of the rating. For example the Teen rating states that a game is suitable for teens. That's the game's rating. A statement on the back of the box, such as "violence, and language," is the descriptor. I've included the ratings below for your perusing pleasure, quoting from the ESRB's web site:

EC (Early Childhood)

Has content that may be suitable for ages 3 and older. Contains no material that parents would find inappropriate.

E (Everyone)

Has content that may be suitable for persons ages 6 and older. Titles in this category may contain minimal violence, some comic mischief and/or mild language.

T (Teen)

Has content that may be suitable for persons ages 13 and older. May contain violent content, mild or strong language, and/or suggestive themes.

M (Mature)

Has content that may be suitable for persons ages 17 and older. Titles in this category may contain mature sexual themes, more intense violence and/or strong language.

Preface

Up and
Running

Maximizing
Your Xbox
Experience

Networking
the Xbox

Take it
Online with
Xbox Live

Xbox
Accessories

Xbox
Buyer's Guide

The Future
Is Bright

X XBOX

28

AO (Adults Only)

Has content suitable only for adults. Titles in this category may include graphic depictions of sex and/or violence. Adult Only products are not intended for persons under the age of 18.

RP (Rating Pending)

Has been submitted to the ESRB and is awaiting final rating.

Parents, you can optimize your child-rearing environment by using the Xbox's parental control feature. It allows you to choose the maximum ESRB rating that may be played on your Xbox. To access the feature, choose Parental Control under Settings. This pops up three options: Set Pass Code (so the kids can't veto your decision after you go to bed), Movies, and Games. You may make your pass code using the controls on your gamepad.

The Xbox's parental control settings

To choose a movie rating, highlight Movies and press the A button. Select the upper limit of the rating you want viewable on your Xbox. Kids, I'd recommend PG, it keeps your parents from using your machine to watch all their naughty PG-13 and R-rated movies.

Setting the movies rating on the Xbox

To set the game ratings, highlight the Games menu, and then choose an upper limit to the games you want to play. That's all there is to it.

Setting the games rating on the Xbox

Get the best sound

Games just aren't as much fun without sound blasting from your TV's speakers. Without sound, you'll still be able to hear your spouse ask you to take out the garbage or the kids plead for help with their homework, and your whole gaming experience will be ruined. Aside from duct-taping their mouths or locking them all in the closet, there are a handful of ways to maximize the sound from your new Xbox: first your can minimize the distractions in the environment, and second, you can maximize the sound coming from the box.

Minimizing distractions

It doesn't really matter how good your sound system is if you can't hear it. Funny thing is that you're not always aware of *when* you can't hear it. Now I'm not recommending you shush everyone in the room when the Xbox comes on, not by a long shot. The reason that consoles rule the world is their social dimension. It's a blast to sit on the couch with your family, playing *Madden 2005*, egging each other on to greatness. But there are times when you want to catch every bit of obscure dialogue, listen for the footsteps of a "tango," or just enjoy the sounds that make a game better. And hey, don't forget that after you've installed the DVD playback adapter, your Xbox becomes a home theater (well, kinda . . . there's no popcorn included). When such a time is at hand, or any other time, try the following suggestions.

Reduce ambient noise

Seems obvious, but I guess reading it in a book makes it official. Does your ceiling fan whir? Oil it. Dog bark? Let him in. Refrigerator hum? Shut it off . . . well, best not do that, something has to keep the beverages cold. But seriously, anything that makes a low, constant noise detracts from your movie or game's sound. The chief culprits are window air conditioning

Preface

Up and
Running

Maximizing
Your Xbox
Experience

Networking
the Xbox

Take it
Online with
Xbox Live

Xbox
Accessories

Xbox
Buyer's Guide

The Future
Is Bright

X XBOX

30

units, ceiling fans, and dishwashers. If you don't need them, turn them off. You'll hear the game better and save electricity to boot.

Clear your ears

You'd be amazed at how much better you'll hear when the sound has a clear path to your ears. Now, I'm not talking about taking a swab to your auditory canals, but rather sitting in a chair that doesn't block your ears. My daughter loves to plop in the biggest, softest chair in the TV room to game. Then she turns up the television to one notch past blaring. The point is that she can't hear the television well because the chair's pillows curve around her head, blocking the sound.

Place your speakers wisely

This isn't an option if your speakers are part of your TV, but many people own separate home theater systems with multiple speakers. Here are some basic guidelines (you can find much more advice at the Crutchfield Advisor: www.crutchfieldadvisor.com).

Center speakers

The center speaker's job is to provide the mainstream sounds—such as dialogue—to the players or viewers. This is the most important speaker in your array of speakers and as such should be placed directly in front of the players or viewers.

Left/right speakers

The left and right speakers should be placed approximately 30 degrees to the left and right of the center speaker. These speakers handle most of your game's music, and include both woofer (low end) and tweeter (high-end) speakers. Position these speakers so that the tweeters are on ear level as you sit to play the game. With larger speakers—approximately 3' tall—floor placement works fine. If your speakers are small, you'll need to place them on a stand. Although these speakers are placed at an angle

Preface

Up and
Running

Maximizing
Your Xbox
Experience

Networking
the Xbox

Take it
Online with
Xbox Live

Xbox
Accessories

Xbox
Buyer's Guide

The Future
Is Bright

✕ xbox

32

to the player's position, they should be the same distance from the player as the center speakers.

Surround Speakers

Your surround speakers should be placed approximately 90 degrees or more to the left and right of the center speaker. These speakers' job is to surround you with diffuse sound. To throw your ears—hopefully, with the rest of your body attached—into the middle of the movie or game. Mount the speakers on the wall, about ear level when you are standing. Do not point the speakers directly at the gamer's or viewer's position. Doing so might overwhelm the front speakers. Remember, the surround speakers should envelop you with sound, not blast you off of your couch with it.

This is the optimum speaker placement.
Notice the surround speakers are 90+
degrees from the center speaker.

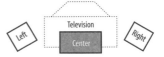

Of course to enjoy all this surround sound stuff, you'll need to have a sound system capable of handling it. There are plenty on the market, from Creative Labs GigaWorks S750 to Kenwood's HTB-S715DV Gaming Home Theater System that not only has six speakers, but headphone support that allows you to game while the rest of the family is listening to a CD. Is that cool or what? I take a closer look at the Xbox's sound system accessories in Chapter 5.

Got game?

Unfortunately, I can't teach you how to "get game" in the few pages available here. I've been gaming—in one form or another—since the early sixties. I love it, but I'm hardly good at it. Games, especially action-type games, require a heck of a lot of practice to master. There are, however, some basic tips I garnered by writing forty-some strategy guides. To some folks, these tips will be obvious, but for others not so much.

No symbols in this shot of EA Sports'
FIFA 2004, but they do pop up

First and foremost, learn the daggone game. It might seem obvious, but I can't tell you how many folks I've met who don't know how to switch weapons in *MechAssault*, use a smoke grenade in *Full Spectrum Warrior*, or what that blue "X" means over the player's heads in *FIFA 2004*. We all like to pull the game out of the box, pop in the tray, and get playing. In fact, if you can't do just that *and* have some fun with it, it's a poor game design. Nevertheless, after you've played for a while, it's a good idea to sit down with the user manual and really learn how the game works. After you do that, you'll be ready for the following tips.

Preface

Up and
Running

Maximizing
Your Xbox
Experience

Networking
the Xbox

Take it
Online with
Xbox Live

Xbox
Accessories

Xbox
Buyer's Guide

The Future
Is Bright

✕ XBOX

34

Strategy and role-playing games

To steal a phrase from the famous Confederate cavalry commander, Nathan Bedford Forest: all strategy games come down to one thing, getting there "the firstest, with the mostest." It doesn't really matter how that happens, but if you stick to that precept, you'll win more than you lose. For example in *Gladius*, you need to get to the critical juncture on the battlefield—whether it is a crate or a bridge—with more gladiators than your opponent, and then use those superior forces to defeat the enemy. Always look for the unfair fight. Look for a way to pit your overwhelming force ("the mostest") against a small portion of your opponent's ("the leastest"). This applies equally well whether playing a turn-based game, such as *Gladius*, or something real-time, like *Aliens vs. Predator: Extinction*. You must still move overwhelming force to the critical point in the battlefield and defeat your enemy.

Colonial Marines in
Electronic Arts' *Aliens vs.
Predator: Extinction*

Winning role-playing games—at least the combat portion of role-playing games—requires a similar strategy. If you're playing with more than one character, use all of them to attack one bad guy until he is eliminated and then move on to the next. Furthermore, always attack the *baddest* bad guy first—you know, the opponent that can do the most damage to your party. Take him or her down first, and the rest will be easy, or at least not so hard.

Oh yeah, if you are playing a role-playing game, buy a strategy guide. Nothing is more frustrating than getting lost, finding an unsolvable puzzle, or running up against an unbeatable boss monster. The strategy guide's author has already suffered that frustration so you won't have to. Use a strategy guide and you'll spend more time having fun and less time grinding your teeth.

Action games

Obviously, winning action strategies depend on the type of game. In *Doom 3* you must have a quick trigger finger, and a sixth sense for what *might* happen when you enter a new room. In *Doom 3*, as in any shooter, it is also important that you constantly move. Standing still, whether in the *MechAssault* series or *Doom 3* is a fast ride to the grave. The trick is to shoot, move, shoot—or even better—shoot while you are moving. The best way to accomplish this is with the *circle strafe*. Circle strafing is a technique in which gamers press the lateral movement joystick, while using the direction stick to keep their aiming crosshair locked on the target. This allows a player to circle his target, presenting a constantly moving target to his enemy while keeping the cursor on—and the lead/laser bolts pumping into—their opponent.

For example in *Halo*, press the left joystick left while pressing the right joystick right. This moves the Master Chief to the left as he is constantly turning right. Hence he cuts a circle around the target as he keeps his crosshairs pointed at it. Speed varies with the pressure you put on the joysticks, so you'll need to experiment with how much you press in a given direction to get this move right.

X xbox

In Activision's *Doom 3*, you best be
careful how you fight these guys

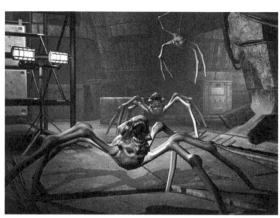

Arcade and racing games

In action games of the racing and arcade variety there is little substitute for
great hand-to-eye coordination. But even great reflexes won't necessarily put
you on top in a realistic racing simulation such as *Moto GP*. It's not a bad idea
to watch some Superbike races on ESPN or Speed, and see how the real racers
do it. There's more to getting around a race track than mashing the A button.
Racers use what they call the racing line (cutting across corners on turns, thus
taking a shorter path than either the outer or inner curve would afford). Watch
a Superbike or Formula One race, and you'll see what I mean.

With fighting games, such as *Capcom Vs SNK2 EO*, once again the key is
practice . . . practice and smarts. Learn each fighter's moves, and how to best
employ them, and as with shooters, you need to keep moving to win. A station-
ary fighter is a knocked-out fighter.

03

Networking the Xbox

At its silicon-based heart, the Xbox is just a Pentium III 733 MHz computer with some robust—well, robust for 2001—upgrades, including an Ethernet (networking) adapter. And, like all computers with Ethernet, the Xbox can be plugged into a network, whether it is a network with other Xbox consoles or a PC network. Why would you want to do that? Several reasons, the chief one being multiplayer gaming. Sure, your Xbox comes with ports for four controllers, but each of the players plugged into your Xbox sees their game on a portion of the same TV screen. Put two players in the game and you get a screen split in two, four players cuts the screen into quarters. While this can still be a blast, it can also be distracting.

Preface

Up and
Running

Maximizing
Your Xbox
Experience

Networking
the Xbox

Take it
Online with
Xbox Live

Xbox
Accessories

Xbox
Buyer's Guide

The Future
Is Bright

X xbox

38

Two-way *Halo*, Microsoft;
playing on a split screen can
get a bit cramped

Enter the networked dragon. Get it? That's like a play on words from that old *Enter the Dragon* film, but sometimes this whole humor thing doesn't work, and a network looks more like a hydra than a dragon anyhow, so let's just get on with the networking, shall we? Folks playing on networked Xbox consoles typically play one per screen (but split-screen mode works with networked Xboxes), and one per screen is much more fun and much less distracting. There are other things that you can do with your networked Xbox, and I cover them here, but before you can do anything at all you must get that box on the network.

Only games that are multiplayer capable can be played by more than one player, and not all of those games may be played via system link (for example, a LAN). Check the back of your game case for the number of players and type of multiplayer your game supports.

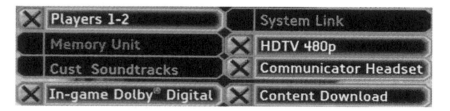

Check the back of your case for the number of players that it supports

Last point . . . networking isn't for everybody. Even though the software in the Xbox is designed to automatically configure the console to your network, it doesn't always happen, and sometimes it can be a bit more trouble than it's worth. But when it works, it works famously. And remember that the Xbox is portable, so combine that with a portable TV, a few like-minded, Xbox-equipped friends, and you have a LAN party. And that is more fun than a barrel of monkeys. (And is that *really* as much fun as they say?)

Preface

Up and
Running

Maximizing
Your Xbox
Experience

Networking
the Xbox

Take it
Online with
Xbox Live

Xbox
Accessories

Xbox
Buyer's Guide

The Future
Is Bright

╳ XBOX

40

Head-to-head network setup

There are a few things that you need before you can connect your Xbox to a network, but exactly what you need depends on what you want to do with your console. No matter what you do, you'll be plugging *something* into your Xbox's Ethernet port.

The Xbox Ethernet port

Xbox to Xbox

This is a straight connection or patch between two Xbox consoles and is the simplest connection to make. But to be honest, none of this is rocket science. To mate two Xboxes together you just need sufficient length of *Category 5 crossover cable* (or "cat 5" for short) to connect the two boxes.

> A Category 5 crossover cable is a cable consisting of four twisted pairs of copper wire terminated by RJ45 connectors. The connectors look like ultra-fat phone connectors.

Plug a connector into each Xbox and you are ready. If you want to use official Xbox hardware, Microsoft makes a system link cable. It comes ready to go with the connectors attached. It's that sexy black color too, which looks much better on, say . . . Kate Beckinsale in *Underworld*, but also works on cables.

Now all you need to do is plop two copies of a system link compatible game into your two Xbox consoles and you are off to the races, fights, war, or whatever. It's important to understand that not all multiplayer-capable Xbox games are system-link compatible. As shown earlier, each game lists its capabilities on the back of its case. If the System Link box doesn't have an "X" next to it, it's not a system link game. You'll also need to keep in mind that it will take *two* copies of the same system link–compatible game to play head-to-head.

If there isn't an "X" beside System Link,
you're out of luck

Xbox-to-computer

You can also use the system link cable (or a generic crossover cable) to hook one Xbox to a computer that has an Ethernet adapter. The Xbox can then access Xbox Live through the computer's broadband connection (see "Share your PC's connection," later).

> In fact, you can access Xbox Live through your computer's dial-up connection. Microsoft doesn't recommend this because it takes some serious bandwidth to run a 16-bike *MotoGP* race with everyone talking via their headset. Nevertheless, there are some games, such as *MechAssault* with which it works just fine. In fact, it's the only way some of us country folks can get on Xbox Live.

Do it LAN party style

Two players are great, but ten are better, and sixteen better still. And yes, the Xbox can support 16 players on a LAN. To hook all these systems up, however, you'll need slightly more equipment than a simple Xbox-to-Xbox or Xbox-to-PC hookup. Hooking to multiple players requires a switch—but a router, (which is basically a switch that can also bridge you to the outside world) will also work, and you'll need one Category 5 patch cable for each Xbox. You can replace the switch with a hub, which is like a switch, but doesn't have as much intelligence when it comes to moving data efficiently.

> If you're setting up a private LAN party, it doesn't matter whether you use a hub, switch, or router. However, if you're going to connect to Xbox Live, you will need a router or a direct connection to the Internet.

Beware; patch cable looks almost identical to crossover cable. The best way to make sure that you have the correct cable is to stride into your local tech store and ask for Ethernet cable.

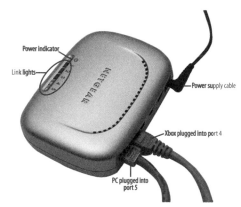

Power indicator

Link lights

Power supply cable

Xbox plugged into port 4

PC plugged into port 5

A five-port Ethernet switch; the link lights blink when there is activity on a given port

After you get the switch and the Ethernet cable, the job is a snap. Hook all the Xboxes into the switch. The Ethernet switch allows them to see each other. Slap a system link multiplayer game into each Xbox, follow the game instructions, and you are off to the races.

As I mentioned in "Xbox to Xbox," you may also plug your Ethernet cable into a switch that is connected to a PC and access Xbox Live through the PC's broadband (or speedy dial-up) connection. The Xbox software can automatically configure the Xbox, but if you are familiar with LANs and the way they work you can also make and change those configurations manually. Either way, I explain how to do both in the next sections.

Preface

Up and
Running

Maximizing
Your Xbox
Experience

Networking
the Xbox

Take it
Online with
Xbox Live

Xbox
Accessories

Xbox
Buyer's Guide

The Future
Is Bright

✕ xᴇox

44

Use a wireless network

Wireless networks are rapidly gaining popularity. The reasons are obvious: No messy wires running along the ceilings or floors of your home, and the mobility that a wireless network provides. For example, a laptop connected to a wireless network allows its user to access the network from anywhere in the house. Although an Xbox lacks the portability of a laptop, it is nice to do away with all those cables. If you decide you want to include your Xbox in your wireless network, you need a Microsoft Wireless adapter for each Xbox that you wish to connect to the network. You can even connect the Xboxes to each other—now is that cool or what?

To plug in to your wireless network, just plug the Microsoft Wireless Adapter into the Xbox, allow the Xbox to automatically configure itself, and you are good to go.

The Microsoft Wireless Adapter

Xbox Live network setup

The ideal configuration for Xbox Live is an Xbox, a broadband Internet connection such as DSL or Cable, and something to connect the two. If you've got more than one PC at home, you've probably already got a home network set up, with a router (perhaps wireless) plugged into your broadband connection. The router distributes the broadband connection to all the computers and devices in your house. If this is the case, plug the Xbox into your router (or use the Wireless Adapter to make this connection without wires).

If you've just got one PC at home, chances are very good that your PC is connected directly to your broadband connection. If so, then you have two choices: use the PC to share its connection to the Xbox, or install a home network.

After you set up your network, you can check out Chapter 4 for more information on Xbox Live.

Share your PC's connection

Most computers come with one Ethernet port. And if you've got this plugged into your broadband connection, you won't be able to use it to connect to your Xbox. Fortunately, an extra Ethernet port can be bought in the form of an add-on PCI card (for desktop users) or an add-on PC Card (for laptop users). Either can be found in your local computer store (and many office supply stores such as Staples or OfficeMax) for under $50.

> Some broadband connections are made over a USB port or through a specialized add-on card. And of course, dial-up users won't be using their Ethernet port for the connection. What it comes down to is this: if your PC's Internet connection is working, and you have an unused and functioning Ethernet port, you can plug your Xbox into it.

Preface

Up and
Running

Maximizing
Your Xbox
Experience

Networking
the Xbox

Take it
Online with
Xbox Live

Xbox
Accessories

Xbox
Buyer's Guide

The Future
Is Bright

X XBOX

46

Here's a desktop with one built-in Ethernet port,
and one provided by an add-on PCI card

Patch cable   Crossover cable
to broadband   to Xbox
connection

Here's a desktop system with two built-in Ethernet
ports — no extra purchase needed!

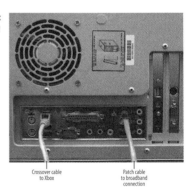

Crossover cable   Patch cable
to Xbox   to broadband
connection

You can even share a WiFi connection: suppose your laptop connects to a
wireless access point that's connected to your broadband connection. You can
share that connection through your laptop's Ethernet port. There are lots of
possibilities!

Here's a laptop system with one WiFi PC Card and one Ethernet port. Use the WiFi to connect to broadband, and share the broadband love through your Ethernet port.

WiFi card connected to wireless home network

Crossover cable to Xbox

To share your connection with your Xbox under Windows XP:

❶ Make sure your PC's Internet connection is working.

❷ If needed, install an extra Ethernet port and configure it according to the manufacturer's instructions.

❸ Plug one end of your System Link cable (or a crossover cable) into the unused Ethernet port on the PC, and the other into the Xbox Ethernet port.

❹ In Windows, click Start → My Network Places. Select "Set Up a Home or Small Office Network" from the list of tasks.

❺ The Network Setup Wizard appears. Click Next.

❻ Review the checklist that appears, and click Next.

❼ The next screen asks you to choose a statement that best describes your computer. Select "This computer connects directly to the Internet. The other computers on my network connect to the Internet through this computer." Click Next.

❽ On the next screen, select the connection that you use to reach the Internet, and click Next.

❾ The next screen asks for a description and name; supply this information and click Next.

⑩ The next screen asks for a workgroup name. You can use the default (MSHOME) and click Next.

⑪ In the screen that comes up next, the wizard asks if you want to enable file sharing. Choose Turn off file and printer sharing. It is not needed for the Xbox. Click Next.

⑫ Finally, you're asked to review the settings and can click Back if you need to change anything. Otherwise, click Next to continue. When it's done, the wizard asks if you want to create a network setup disk. It's okay to say Just finish the wizard here.

⑬ If asked whether you want to reboot your computer now, click yes.

My . . . er, your Network Places on a Windows XP PC

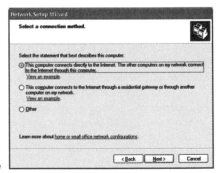

Tell the wizard how you want things done

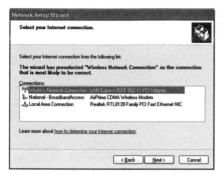

Choose the connection you want to share; this should be the connection that's connected to your broadband or dial-up service

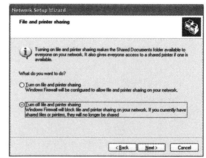

You can leave file and print sharing disabled; your Xbox doesn't need it

Create a home network

If you don't have a home network, now is a good time to consider setting one up. Even if you are a dial-up user, you can get plenty of mileage out of a home network. A home network has the following elements:

Connection to the outside world

This is usually a broadband connection, but can also be dial-up.

Preface

Up and
Running

Maximizing
Your Xbox
Experience

Networking
the Xbox

Take it
Online with
Xbox Live

Xbox
Accessories

Xbox
Buyer's Guide

The Future
Is Bright

X xBOX

Connections to the inside world

This comes in the form of a switch or a wireless access point. Sometimes the functions are combined into one device. The purpose of the switch and/or access point is to allow your computers and devices (including your Xbox) to talk to one another.

A router

This is the bridge between the computers and devices on your network and the outside world. Quite often, the functions of a router, switch, and a wireless access point are rolled into one device. Most routers also provide firewall capabilities, which helps keep malicious hackers on the outside of your network, where they belong.

Xbox Live can run into some problems with un-supported routers. This can take the form of everything from Xbox Live not working at all to reduced Xbox Live functionality. For the gory details, see Microsoft's "Diagnosing Xbox Live Connections with the Xbox Dashboard" document at *www.xbox.com/en-us/live/connect/diagnosing.htm*. You can find a list of Microsoft-approved routers at *www.xbox.com/en-US/live/connect/routerlanding.htm*.

Some wireless router/switch combos, such as the D-Link DI-824VUP, have a serial port you can connect to an external modem. They call it a "backup dial-up modem," but it's a good choice for dial-up users who want to cut the cord between their computers and the phone jack.

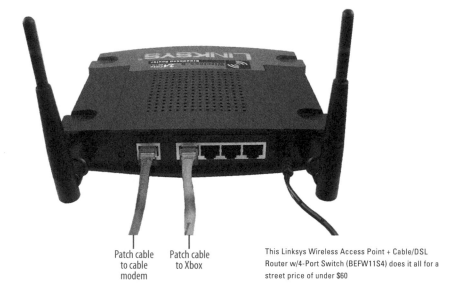

Patch cable to cable modem

Patch cable to Xbox

This Linksys Wireless Access Point + Cable/DSL Router w/4-Port Switch (BEFW11S4) does it all for a street price of under $60

If you had your PC plugged directly into your broadband connection before you installed your home network router, you may need to *power cycle* (turn off, wait about a minute, turn back on) your broadband equipment (such as a cable or DSL Modem) before it will work. The reason for this is that many cable and DSL modems "lock" themselves to the first device they see when they are first turned on. As a result, if you put a home network router between your PC and your cable/DSL modem, it will need to be power cycled before it can lock itself to your router.

Configure your network

Those of you who have fiddled with networks will be ecstatic to see how easy it is to get an Xbox plugged into a network. There are two ways to do it: automatic and manual. The beauty of the Xbox software is that the automatic configuration almost always works. Nevertheless, I also touch on how to configure the Xbox networking manually.

Everyone likes stuff that is automatic. Our lives are tough enough as it is, we don't need any more hassle, and with that in mind, Microsoft came up with automatic configuration. Automatic configuration is a snap. From the Xbox Dashboard (the screen that pops onto your television when you start the Xbox without a game in the tray), choose Settings.

As I discuss in the first chapter, this is where you configure your Xbox; it is also where you set up the network setting. Choose Network from the available menu.

Now we get to the real hardcore stuff. The next menu has four choices: IP Addresses, DNS Servers, PPOE Settings, and Advanced. Although this stuff might seem complicated, it isn't, and the automatic configuration makes it even less so. First, let's look at manual configuration.

Preface

Up and
Running

Maximizing
Your Xbox
Experience

Networking
the Xbox

Take it
Online with
Xbox Live

Xbox
Accessories

Xbox
Buyer's Guide

The Future
Is Bright

X XBOX

52

Manual configuration

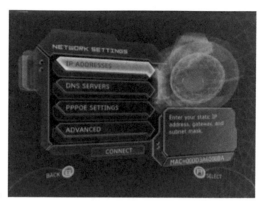

The Network settings Menu

Select IP addresses and press the A button. This brings up the IP Address screen. An IP Address is just a numeric address that labels a computer, Xbox, or other device. It tells the other systems on the LAN who and where it is. There are four settings you can enter on this screen:

IP Address

> If you know which addresses are in use on your network, and you have an unused address, set this to Manual and specify the unused IP address. Be sure to not assign that address to any other computer, Xbox, or other networked device.

Subnet Mask

> The subnet mask helps to further delineate the computer's address. On most networks, a subnet mask of 255.255.255.0 works just fine.

Preface

Up and
Running

Maximizing
Your Xbox
Experience

Networking
the Xbox

Take it
Online with
Xbox Live

Xbox
Accessories

Xbox
Buyer's Guide

The Future
Is Bright

✕ XBOX

Gateway

The gateway is the IP address of the computer or router that your computer uses to access the Internet. You may get this information from your Internet Service Provider (ISP), or it may be available in the configuration application for your home networking router.

PPOE

Point-to-Point Protocol over Ethernet specifies how your Xbox interacts with a broadband modem to log onto the Internet (in this case Xbox Live). It relies on Ethernet and the point-to-point protocol (PPP), and is no more difficult to set up than the typical Internet connection (type in the username and password supplied by your ISP).

Simple, isn't it? But not as simple as what I'll explain in the next section.

Automatic configuration

Rather than go through all that number selection—I mean let's face it, without a keyboard, it's a pain in the neck—why not let your Xbox do it for you? After all, you paid good money for the thing, why not put it to work? From the IP Addresses menu, select Automatic. The Xbox will search your LAN, discover the information that it needs, and apply it appropriately. In less time than it took to describe it, you'll be hooked up to the LAN, and raring to go.

The network settings also allows you to access and set up alternate DNS Servers, and enter settings needed to access your ISP, but none of that should normally be needed. Just choose Automatic, and away you go.

The wireless LAN

Connecting to a wireless LAN is just as painless. First, make sure than you have the Microsoft's Wireless Adapter installed and your wireless LAN is on. Next, choose the Advanced Option from the Network Settings menu. Three settings reside on the Advanced Menu: Wireless, Host Name, and Mac Address. You only need to worry about Wireless.

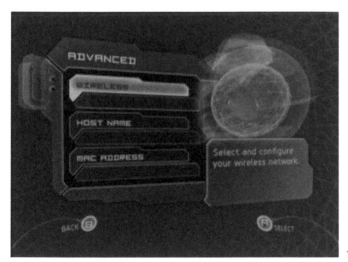

The Wireless option

Select Wireless and the Xbox will detect your wireless LAN's settings and automatically configure your Xbox. No fuss, no muss.

The invisible Xbox

X XBOX

Okay, your Xbox is on the network. You know that it's on the network because you are connecting to Xbox Live through your computer's Internet connection. You know it is on the network because if the Xbox couldn't see the network it wouldn't have been able to hook up. Yet despite this knowledge, when you go to My Network Places on your PC you can't see the Xbox. Why?

Well, the answer is really simple. Unless you own the developer version of the Xbox—and these are *very* hard to get—Microsoft doesn't want you messing with the files on the Xbox, hence Microsoft has limited what your Xbox does on the LAN to accessing the Internet through your PC or playing games with other Xboxes. So, you can't access the Xbox's files the way that you can access files on other computers. That's not so bad, the Xbox plays fine without any tinkering, but if you want to find out more about how you can tinker with your Xbox, visit www.xboxhacker.com.

04

Take It Online with Xbox Live

There are a ton of great games for the Xbox. From *Madden 2005* to *Riddick: Escape* from *Butcher Bay*, you can play in just about any universe that you desire. But after you have played and beaten the universe, the real fun begins. No matter how ingenious a game's artificial intelligence may be, no matter how clever the traps the designers have laid for you, no matter how difficult the puzzles you may solve, nothing compares to the challenge and satisfaction of defeating the grocer down the street or even a stranger from London.

Of course Xbox slaps a steaming heap of multiplayer options on your plate. The simplest is the split-screen 2-4 controller option. As you saw in Chapter 3, when your game is multiplayer capable, just plug in two controllers to the same Xbox and follow the multi-player instructions. You'll end up with something that looks like the figure below.

THQ's Moto GP lets two players race on the same screen against each other

Of course, you may also hook two Xboxes together with the System Link cable, and play against your buddy in the immense glory of full screen, or you can use the LAN to connect up to 16 Xboxes together and have about the most fun known to mankind. Make sure, however, that you check the back of the game box before you plan your LAN party. You can plug in all the Xboxes that your heart desires but you still won't be able to get a multiplayer game going with Electronic Art's excellent strategy game *Aliens vs. Predator: Extinction*—it *doesn't support* multiplayer.

Great game, but there isn't any multiplayer

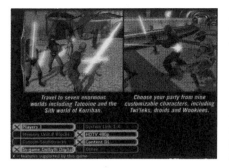

Travel to seven enormous worlds including Tatooine and the Sith world of Korriban.

Choose your party from nine customizable characters, including Twi'leks, droids and Wookiees.

Always check on the back of the box for the game features. It may save you a lot of heartache.

The back of Microsoft's *Knights of the Old Republic* box tells you that it is a one player game, has Dolby Digital sound, is HDTV compliant, and has downloads available (Content DL) on Xbox Live... but it won't do multiplayer.

There is, however, one problem with split screen, system cable, and LAN hookups. No matter how many Xboxes you have hooked together, you need some people to compete against. For some of you—those living in or near big cities, this will be little or no problem. For some others, getting like-minded friends together for some multiplayer Xbox gaming can be a real chore. But not on Xbox Live. There are gamers from all over the world just waiting for you to log on so they can kick your tail in a friendly game of *MechAssault* or *Doom 3*.

I knew it! These folks have just been waiting here to kick my behind.

So, what are you waiting for? Read on and find out how to hook up, log on, and join the fun.

Start with a starter kit

Is the Xbox ready for Xbox Live right out of the box? Well, it is and it isn't. Certainly the hardware is ready for some fun, but you'll need a starter kit to hook up to Xbox Live. The kits comes in several different flavors, and Microsoft is constantly changing what they have to offer, so check your nearest authorized Xbox retailer (just about every store that sells console games or electronics) or log on to www.xbox.com/en-US/hardware/xboxliveservice.htm and find the package that is right for you. One thing that all the starter kits have in common is a subscription code—you'll need this to activate your account.

This is one example of an Xbox Starter Kit

Note that not all starter kits come with a *communicator* (Xbox parlance for a headset). You *must* have a communicator. Sure you can still play without it, but you won't have as much fun. Remember the Xbox doesn't have a keyboard for chatting, if you want to talk smack—or even if you want to talk nicely—you'll need the communicator.

Preface

Up and Running

Maximizing Your Xbox Experience

Networking the Xbox

Take it Online with Xbox Live

Xbox Accessories

Xbox Buyer's Guide

The Future Is Bright

X xbox

60

Get connected

Okay, once you have that starter kit, you are ready to go, right? Wrong. Make sure that you are hooked into a broadband connection. Chapter 3 has extensive information on hooking up to a LAN or broadband connection, as well as sharing your PC's connection with your Xbox.

Get logged on

Now you are ready to go, all you need to do is follow the prompts and you'll soon be gaming online. Just in case you have any questions, let's go through the new account and logon process.

After you have it set up, the Xbox Live Dashboard looks something like this; your mileage may vary depending on the starter kit you purchased

Before you can sign up for a new account, you'll need to—as Microsoft puts it—update the Xbox Dashboard. As you probably remember, the Dashboard is the main menu that pops when you start up your Xbox. There are two ways to perform this update: insert your spanking new starter kit disc, or insert an Xbox Live–capable game, and select Xbox Live from its menu.

From the next menu, you'll need to choose to start a new account . . . duh. I mean if you already had an account, you wouldn't need to go through all of this would you? If you did have an account you would see the screen shown here.

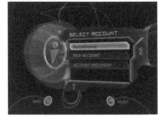

This is the first screen you'll see after selecting Xbox Live

The next screen to pop up is a welcome screen with the conditions of service. Read them and tap the A button when you are done. The following screens are self-explanatory: they'll ask for your billing region, provide the terms of use, prompt you to choose your Gamertag (a nickname that you choose, such as "deadlybunny"), date of birth, the subscription code (found on the card in the starter kit, scratch off silver to reveal code), and credit card information. My first suggestion is to take your time. You aren't working with a keyboard, and it's very easy to mess up an entry, which may necessitate restarting. Hint number two—choose a cool screen name. I chose my actual name and felt like a dork fighting Dark Master, Kung Fu Lightning, and other cool names online.

After you have registered, you'll be able to select Xbox Live from the opening Xbox Dashboard. Doing so displays a screen with the following options:

YourName

Actually, instead of *YourName*, it displays your account name (also known as your Gamertag). This takes you to your Xbox Live account.

New Account

Use this if you want to set up a new account.

Recover Account

Use this option if you need to recover an account that is no longer working. The Xbox will attempt to automatically restore the account settings.

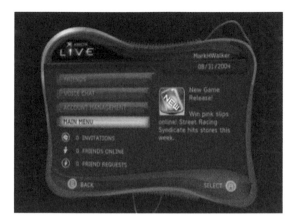

This screen presents several options for managing your account

Manage your account

To manage your account, choose Xbox Live from the Dashboard, and then select your Gamertag from the list; this displays the following information that lets you manage your account.

Friends

Met someone online that you like? Select Friends, and then enter their Gamertag on the subsequent screen. This will send an invitation to them to become your friend. If they accept, they'll be listed when you click on Friends. The lower part of the screen will also let you know how many friends you have online, how many invitations you have to become someone's friend and how many friend requests you have out. You may invite friends to play by simply selecting their name and sending the invite. Your friend's status—for example, whether they are online, have their communicator turned on, and so forth—is indicated by an icon

Maximizing Your Xbox Experience

Take it Online with Xbox Live

The Future Is Bright

beside their name. You'll also see similar icons in game lobbies.

Here's what they mean:

 This friend is on your list, and currently logged on to Xbox Live.

 You've sent a friend request to this person. No answer yet. Keep your fingers crossed.

 You've received a friend request. This means that you are *very* popular and will go on to do big things in your life.

 The person's communicator is on. They are ready to talk some smack.

 This person's communicator is off.

 This person doesn't have a communicator.

 You've sent this friend a game invitation.

 You've received a game invitation.

Voice Chat

As the name would imply, this is where you go to do a bit of chatting. You'll need to have a communicator to do so. When you press this button, you'll be taken to the screen shown in the following figure. Online friends appear here. Choose one to chat with and start talking. Pressing the Y buttons brings up a couple of options. You may choose to have your

friends' voices piped through your speakers and decide whether you want to appear online or not. If you choose not, no one else can see that you are online.

The Voice Chat "room"

Whether in the chat room or in a game lobby, some folks can get a bit obnoxious. You may mute them by selecting their name, pressing the A button, and selecting Voice: Off. Turn them on again by selecting Voice: On.

Account Management

Selecting this option whisks you away to the account management screen. From the account management screen you may change your pass code or the credit card with which you pay for your subscription, view and alter your subscription and the account settings (including whether you wish your account to be voice enabled, whether you can download premium content, and content created by other Xbox players), review the Xbox live policies, and set exactly whom you wish to share your account information with (Microsoft and/or partners).

Preface

Up and
Running

Maximizing
Your Xbox
Experience

Networking
the Xbox

Take it
Online with
Xbox Live

Xbox
Accessories

Xbox
Buyer's Guide

The Future
Is Bright

X xbox

66

You can take your account information with you on the
Microsoft Memory Card. By doing so, you may plug the
card in your aunt's (or whoever) controller, and you are
ready to sign on Xbox live.

The Microsoft Memory Card

Return to the main menu
This takes you back to the main menu.

Get the most from your game

The options above are generic Xbox Live options. When you put in an Xbox
Live game, a different set of options appears. Each game is not identical, but
most of them do have some basic choices in common. In all of them you'll
need to select Xbox Live, choose
the account, and enter your pass
code. After doing so you'll be
taken to the game's Xbox Live
lobby, as shown in the following
screenshot.

THQ's *Full Spectrum Warrior* Xbox Live Lobby

Most games provide the following options:

Create Game

Lets you create a game with the parameters that you want. You can decide whether to open the game to the public, keep it private (only your friends can play), enable voice, and numerous other game-specific options.

Quick Game

This throws you into the next game that is starting. It pays no attention to any game parameters you've set. It's a good way to get in some fast action.

Opti-Match

Allows you to look for a game, but only games that meet your preset parameters. For example, perhaps you only like 10-minute *MechAssault* destruction matches. Opti-Match will hunt for one of those. The upside is that you get into games with the parameters you want. The downside is that it's a little harder to find games this way.

My Xbox Live

This allows you to review your friends and see who you've played recently. If you are connected to one of your friends, you can trade saved games, replays, skins, levels, and whatever else the game allows.

Many games, such as *MechAssault,* allow a Gamertag to bring a guest into the game with them. Each player—the account holder and their guest—logs into the game with the account holder's Gamertag. Xbox Live automatically assigns the second player as *Gamertagguest,* where Gamertag is the account holder's Gamertag.

MSN Messenger

Xbox live integrates with MSN Messenger. You can see when your friends are online, get game invitations, new game notifications, and all kinds of stuff. To sign up, all you need do is click the Alert tab on MSN messenger, and follow the sign-up instructions. And as if that wasn't enough, you can even have the alerts or game invitations sent to your mobile cellular device.

Preface

Up and Running

Maximizing Your Xbox Experience

Networking the Xbox

Take it Online with Xbox Live

Xbox Accessories

Xbox Buyer's Guide

The Future Is Bright

✕ XBOX

68

Click the glowing green Xbox Live tab on MSN Messenger

Fill out the requested information

Check the Xbox *Live* Alerts you want to receive:

☑ **Game Invitations.**
Get game invitations, plus reminders about your upcoming tournaments and competitions.

☑ **Friend Requests.**
Receive new Friend Requests or find out when other gamers invite you to join their team or tournament.

☐ **Logon.**
Get a message when anyone on your Friends List logs on to Xbox *Live*.

☑ **Xbox *Live* Service Message.**
Receive important messages about your Xbox *Live* service, such as scheduled maintenance and system updates.

☑ **Xbox *Live* Downloadable Content.**
Find out about new content for your favorite games as soon as it's released.

☑ **Xbox *Live* Game Release.**
Get announcements about hot new games for Xbox *Live*.

☐ **Xbox News and Events.**
Find out about Xbox *Live* events, such as the XSN Sports World Championship.

And then set the alerts that you wish to receive. These display as a pop-up on Messenger. You may also choose delivery method, including having game invites displayed on your cell phone.

You can specify whether alerts should be delivered to your instant messenger client, email account, or mobile device.

The final tip

Be nice. It's easy to get cocky and say mean things to folks on Xbox Live you'll never see again. Refrain from doing so for two reasons. Reason one, if you get a bad rep no one will want to game with you, and reason number two—it's not nice.

05

Xbox Accessories

The Xbox is cool right out of the box, so to speak. You can game, you can link to other Xboxes and—with a starter kit—you can get onto Xbox Live. Yet despite that coolness, there are a ton of other options waiting for you out there in Xboxland, and it only takes an investment in some Xbox accessories to realize them. From cool new controllers to the DVD playback kit, there are tons of accessories that you can plug into your Xbox to enhance your enjoyment of the machine. So, let's take a tour of the best accessories available and learn how to enhance the Xbox gaming experience.

I'll describe these accessories, and tell you the pros and cons. I'll also give you an approximate street price. Your shopping mileage may vary.

Play movies

This is as necessary as it is debated. The PlayStation 2 ships ready to play your DVDs, the Xbox doesn't. On the other hand, the PS2's DVD player is temperamental—if the DVD is slightly scratched, smudged, or too hot, it will skip, chatter, or stop playing. Conversely, the Xbox plays DVDs reliably with the adapter kit. So which system/marketing technique is better? I don't know, but I do know that if you own an Xbox, the DVD adapter is a must-have accessory.

If you own an Xbox, you simply must buy the DVD adapter

The adapter is one of the simplest accessories ever created. Plug it into a controller port, snap two AAA batteries in the remote, and you are ready to go. Keep in mind that the Xbox ships from the factory capable of playing DVDs from *any* region. However, once you have snapped in the adapter, it will play DVDs only from that adapter's region (meaning the region in which the adapter was bought). You will not be able to use an adapter from another region after that.

Preface

Up and Running

Maximizing Your Xbox Experience

Networking the Xbox

Take it Online with Xbox Live

Xbox Accessories

Xbox Buyer's Guide

The Future Is Bright

X xBOX

72

If you are interested in modding your Xbox for other regions you may buy and install a mod chip (www.xbreporter.com lists mod chips on the market). One of the simplest to install seems to be the Messiah chip. It only has 11 wires to solder, and prevents the Xbox from locking onto the region code from the first DVD adapter you plug in it. Accordingly, you can then plug adapters from other regions into the Xbox and play DVDs from other regions. A successfully installed Messiah will also allow you to play import Xbox games and even backup copies. But after you open your Xbox to install the chip, you invalidate its warranty. Is it really worth it? That's up to you.

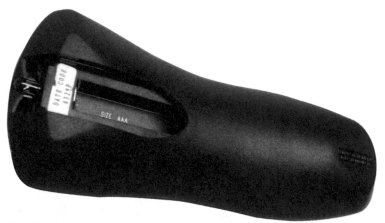

Place AAA batteries in here

Steering wheels

The dominant controller for the Xbox—or any other console for that matter—is the game pad. Many people swear it is the only controller that you'll need, and they daggone well may be right. Nevertheless, racing aficionados, especially those who prefer racing simulations, such as *NASCAR 2005: Chase for the Cup*, often prefer to race their simulation with a steering wheel. The sensation you get from sawing the wheel, mashing the gas, and toeing the brake make it almost feel as if you actually were in a race car.

MadCatz, a console aftermarket giant, has a great steering wheel and pedal set called the MC2 Racing Wheel and Pedals. The steering wheel has a rubberized grip and the pedals feel just about right. For a street price in the neighborhood of $50, it's not a bad deal.

Preface

Up and Running

Maximizing Your Xbox Experience

Networking the Xbox

Take it Online with Xbox Live

Xbox Accessories

Xbox Buyer's Guide

The Future Is Bright

X xbox

74

The MadCatz Racing Wheel

Of course those who want the ultimate racing experience will want to take a look at Bob Earl's Virtual Racing Chassis. Bob Earl was a very successful sports car driver in his day, and he has put that expertise into creating an experience that is the closest you can get to actually being in the cockpit of a racing car.

Bob Earl's Virtual Racing Chassis

Bob has made a frame, seat, and monitor mounting assembly that put you in the same position as a race driver. The "chassis" does not come with its own steering wheel and pedals but is compatible with most brands including the MadCatz Racing Wheel. Sit in this puppy, in front of a large screen, and you'll feel everything race drivers feel, except the price of repairing your damaged car.

> A couple of things to remember when racing with wheels and pedals. Race drivers have a saying, "slow in the cockpit means fast on the track." Driving a race car is a fine art, not an experiment in macho wheel jerking. You'll drive faster, and win more often if you make your movements gentle, measured, and understated. Don't stomp the throttle (accelerator) or jerk the wheel.

You'll win these races more often if you drive smoothly
(Codemaster's *Colin McRae Rally 2005*)

Controllers and light guns

Microsoft makes a great controller that ships with the Xbox—it is responsive, comfortable, and durable. But there are numerous other controllers on the market. I cover only a very small percentage of them here, but you can browse further in your favorite electronic store.

The Radica FPS Master Controller

The Radica FPS Master Controller is probably the final shot (shot, get it?) in first-person shooter controllers. From its science-fiction style, to its never-take-your-thumbs-off-the-joysticks design, this controller is built from the silicon board up to do nothing more than enhance the greatness that is you. It you're serious about your *Halo* or *Doom 3* gaming, this is the controller for your hands.

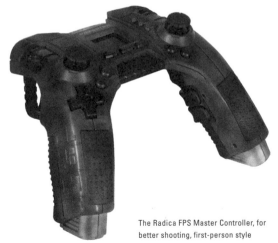

The Radica FPS Master Controller, for better shooting, first-person style

Preface

Up and
Running

Maximizing
Your Xbox
Experience

Networking
the Xbox

Take it
Online with
Xbox Live

Xbox
Accessories

Xbox
Buyer's Guide

The Future
Is Bright

X XBOX

76

Nyko Airflo Ex

This is just so cool. The AirfFlo is like a standard Xbox controller. It has pretty much the same buttons, two triggers, a D-Pad, and a pair of joysticks. What it has that are different are two vents, one in each handle and fans that blow air through them. No more will your best friend's sweaty hands yuck up your controller. The air will keep them cool and your controller dry. It weighs in at approximately $35. Sweet.

The Nyko Airflo Ex; check out the vents

Wireless controllers

My worst gaming nightmare is snagging a foot in the controller wire, dragging the Xbox off the shelf, and ruining my beautiful machine. It happened once before with my PlayStation, and turned the console into an expensive paper weight. Xbox tries to mitigate that danger with their inline release, but nothing in this world is ever sure.

The controller wire inline release. Yank too hard, and this pops apart

✕ xʙox

The only way, however, to truly eliminate the danger is to remove the wire. That is what wireless controllers do. Most wireless controllers will work up to 40 feet from the Xbox. Unless you have a big, and by big I mean *huge*, screen television, that is plenty far away.

Numerous companies, including MadCatz, Logitech, and Intec, make wireless controllers, so finding one should be no problem. Remember, however, that the controllers are battery powered. Most get hundreds of hours with vibration turned off, and tens of hours with it turned on.

A Logitech wireless controller

All wireless controllers currently on the market are incompatible with the Xbox Live controller because they use its port to communicate with the Xbox. But hey, if you don't mind playing without the communicator, it'll work fine on Xbox Live. Conversely, HIP Gear will release a wireless controller with headset in late 2004. That should fit the bill.

Light guns

Some folks get a real thrill out of playing first-person shooters by pointing a weapon at the television and banging away. For these people, several manufacturers market a light gun. The gun sends a signal to the Xbox that conveys

where it is aiming. If you aim correctly, you hit your target. Several companies make these, including Dragon Light and Innovation Technologies.

The Battle Boss Dragon Light Gun

Keep in mind that light guns work only with specially marked light-gun-compatible games (usually prominently displayed on the box). If you hope to blast your way through *Halo*, you'll be disappointed.

Preface

Up and
Running

Maximizing
Your Xbox
Experience

Networking
the Xbox

Take it
Online with
Xbox Live

Xbox
Accessories

Xbox
Buyer's Guide

The Future
Is Bright

X xbox

80

Go fishing, dancing, or whatever

Of course not everyone wants to go racing or shooting. There are those among us who like to go fishing when the weather is bad, or even dancing when it's one in the afternoon.

Catching fish in *Altus Pro Fishing Challenge*

That's okay, the Xbox has you covered. For example, Naki World's Bass Champion Fishing Controller lets you cast for trout without ever leaving the comfort of your couch. MadCatz Beat Pad lies on the floor and records your moves so you can dance with the best of them. Hey, it beats sitting in your easy chair. Or does it?

MadCatz Beat Pad lets you keep the beat

But if you can believe it, the unique types of controllers don't end there. With the rise in popularity of Tony Hawk has come a whole series of skate and snowboarding games for all the consoles. The Xbox is no exception. These games are edge-of-the-seat experiences no matter what type of controller you use, but some enthusiasts won't be happy until they get the best skateboarding experience possible.

Busting a move with Konami's *Dance Dance Revolution Ultramix 2*

That experience is available on the Thrustmaster Freestyler Board. The board comes complete with a one-handed controller. That controller, coupled with the board, provides all the functionality you'll find in a standard Xbox controller.

The Thrustmaster Freestyler

X xbox

82

The old standby

Throughout the years, a simple joystick has come to be associated with gaming more than any other piece of hardware. Although times have not completely passed over the joystick, and in spite of the advent of more sophisticated control systems and the decline of flight simulations and other games that just "feel right" with the joystick, there are still plenty of sticks to be bought, and a lot of gamers that enjoy using them.

If you are one of those gamers, you can choose sticks from a variety of sources. Thrustmaster, MadCatz, and several others all make joysticks for the Xbox with a wide range of features that are sure to suit any gamer's needs.

Joysticks are best for three types of games: Flight, fighting, and stuff like *MechAssault*. If you are a fan of these genres, a joystick is a good investment. But if you are a truly a fan of giant biped weapon platform combat you'll want to pick up a copy of *Steel Battalion*—the ultimate 'Mech game that not only includes a two-joystick, three-pedal, 40-button controller, but *requires* it to play the game.

Take Two Interactive's *Wings of War*

Thrustmaster Top Flight 2 Controller

Cap Con's *Steel Battalion* . . . unbelievable!

Cheating

To quote the vile Captain Barbossa in the *Pirates of the Caribbean*: a game has "more what you'd call guidelines than actual rules." Everyone that has played a computer or console game knows the sick feeling that comes with sinking hours into a game only to find that you have come across a boss that you can't beat, a level that you can't conquer, or a track that you can't race. What to do, what to do?

The answer is simple: cheat. Or at least play somebody else's game. Let me explain. There are a couple of ways to cheat—actually it is the same way, but with different methodology. One way is to go to any number of the online cheat sites (www.cheats.it has a good selection) and see if they have posted any codes for the game on which you want to cheat. Frequently, you need to do no more than press a prescribed selection of D-Pad entries to become invulnerable, or whatever. For example, "For a faster car press: up, down, up, right and black button on city map."

Just use the cheats that you need. Sometimes entering too many cheats can cause the game to crash.

www.cheats.it has an awesome selection of cheats

Preface

Up and
Running

Maximizing
Your Xbox
Experience

Networking
the Xbox

Take it
Online with
Xbox Live

Xbox
Accessories

Xbox
Buyer's Guide

The Future
Is Bright

X xbox

84

Another way is to get some help from software. Some companies, such as Gameshark, offer the same cheat codes (and ones that are even more difficult to enter) on special CD/DVD packages. You plop the disc into your Xbox drive, and then select the game and cheat that you want. It's very little fuss, and absolutely no muss.

Sometimes, however, you'll just want to jump over a difficult or—dare we say, boring—part of a game. Gameshark can also help you there by offering CDs that have saved games (including those with cheats loaded) for many, many popular Xbox games. Now you can jump right in to the middle of *Riddick: Escape from Butcher Bay*, seventh level (or wherever).

Gameshark's saved game discs can really
save you some serious aggravation

Here's how you use the typical Gameshark disc:

❶ The disc package comes with a dongle—the thing that plugs into the front of your controller. Insert the dongle into your controller.

❷ Place the Gameshark disc into your Xbox.

❸ Select the game and the cheats that you wish to use. You may scroll through the menus with the D-Pad and choose the game and cheats with the A button.

Choose the cheat you need

❹ After you have loaded them, remove the disc.

❺ Insert your game disc, and you are ready to go.

Preface

Up and
Running

Maximizing
Your Xbox
Experience

Networking
the Xbox

Take it
Online with
Xbox Live

Xbox
Accessories

Xbox
Buyer's Guide

The Future
Is Bright

✕ xʙox

86

The last accessories

Some accessories don't help you to play better, see or hear the game better, or enhance the game in any way, but are still so cool that they deserve mention. You can keep an eye on the cool new accessories at several web sites including www.xbreporter.com, www.xbox.com, and several others.

MadCatz HDTV Component System Selector

If you have a couple of HDTV input devices, this puppy can save you a lot of work. You plug them into here, and then plug the selector into your TV. Now, all you need to do to switch from your DVD player (for example) to your Xbox is turn the selector dial.

MadCatz HDTV Component System Selector

Xbox Game Manager

This is a great device for cleaning up your Xbox area. It's Xbox-sized (you can stack an Xbox on top), has mounts on the side for two controllers, and a surge

protector and six power outlets. Additionally there is storage provided for multiple Xbox games. It keeps the room clean and your significant other happy. It's made by APC.

Xbox Game Manager

Xbox Buyer's Guide: The Best Games Now and in the Future

You've learned all that I can teach you in this small book. From hooking up the Xbox, to setting up a LAN party, you know it all, but the one thing that I haven't discussed is the Xbox's raison d'etre: games. All the Xbox chops in the world won't do you any good if you don't know the best games to slide into the DVD tray.

That, of course, is where this chapter enters stage right. I can't cover all the Xbox games, or even a small percentage—that would take another (and much larger) book. I can, however, discuss the best the Xbox currently has to offer, and also take a look into the gaming crystal ball at the big games in the Xbox's future. For those of you keeping score, I'm not listing the games in order of goodness, but rather in a secret, contrived order that only makes sense to me. In other words, randomly.

Project Gotham Racing 2

Genre: Racing
Publisher: Microsoft (www.microsoft.com)

Hands down the best racing game for Xbox, and one of the best for any console, *Project Gotham Racing 2* is a gut wrenching combination of realistic physics, white-knuckled street racing, and voluptuous visuals. Developed by Bizarre Creations and published by Microsoft Game Studios, *Project Gotham Racing 2* is unique in that it not only rewards fast drivers, but also drivers who takes risks.

The more daring the line you drive, the better the results, measured in Kudo points. These points may then be utilized to unlock new cars. There are tons of cars from the Mini-Cooper to the Ford GT40, and you may race on tracks all around the world. The physics engine is realistic, but has obviously been tweaked to provide maximum fun with minimum stress. There are several modes you may choose to play. Those hankering for a fast game can jump right in with the instant action mode, while those who favor a more long-term commitment will want to sign up for the Kudos World Series, in which you compete with different classes on all the *Project Gotham Racing 2* tracks, and the socially minded can compete against up to seven other people on Xbox Live.

No matter how you choose to compete, you'll like the game. So, get a wheel, plug it in, and take off.

Preface

Up and Running

Maximizing Your Xbox Experience

Networking the Xbox

Take it Online with Xbox Live

Xbox Accessories

Xbox Buyer's Guide

The Future Is Bright

X XBOX

88

Microsoft's *Project Gotham Racing 2*

Full Spectrum Warrior

Genre: Strategy/Simulation

Publisher: THQ (www.thq.com)

It is rare when something truly unique arrives in the gaming community, and *Full Spectrum Warrior* is such an entity. At first glance the game looks like any number of first-person shooters. Oh, make no mistake, it looks darn good, and has all the trappings of a shooter—realistic visuals, third person perspective, gun battles, the works. The game, however, is not a shooter, but rather a simulation of modern, squad-level combat and tactics.

Initially developed as a trainer for the United States Army, the game takes players through a couple of days in the life a U.S. Army squad as they fight alongside United Nations forces in a struggle to liberate Zekistan. Gamers control the two fire teams that make up the squad, and occasionally a third element, such as engineers or a sniper. You'll also get a chance to work alongside a Bradley Infantry Fighting Vehicle. Gamers can order fire teams to lay down two types of suppressive fire, lob smoke and frag grenades (in addition to firing the 40mm grenades from the M203 grenade launcher), advancing rapidly, or covering each other during an advance.

It's critical to employ realistic tactics, pinning enemies with one team while the other maneuvers to flank and eliminate the opposition. Keeping teams behind cover is important, as is the benefit of cover fire.

THQ's *Full Spectrum Warrior*; Fireteam Alpha
looks for targets.

Preface

Up and Running

Maximizing Your Xbox Experience

Networking the Xbox

Take it Online with Xbox Live

Xbox Accessories

Xbox Buyer's Guide

The Future Is Bright

✕ xbox

The ambiance is stunning. *Full Spectrum Warrior* boasts some of the best graphics found on the Xbox. The soldier animations, terrain, and weapons look almost as good as full-motion animation—the type of computer graphics used in the ground breaking *Final Fantasy* film. The sound effects are equally good, and the soldiers' voice acting—although laced with curse words—is top notch. If you enjoy strategy gaming or military simulations, you'll love *Full Spectrum Warrior*

Knights of the Old Republic

Genre: Role-playing
Publisher: Lucas Arts (www.lucasarts.com)

For many years games based on movie licenses have been somewhat of a joke. Publishers seemed to feel that carrying the *Star Wars, Star Trek, Batman*, or whatever name was enough to ensure success, and to a certain extent they were correct. At first casual gamers snapped up licensed games in droves, happy to play something that thrust them into their favorite universe, but as more and more publishers released trash, fewer and fewer gamers bought them.

But that was then, and this is now. Since the late nineties publishers have gotten serious with their licenses and the extra effort shows. Perhaps the most critically acclaimed of all the licensed games is Lucas Arts' *Knights of the Old Republic (KOTOR)*. A *Star Wars* role-playing game (RPG) developed by Bioware (who also developed the PC-based smash hit *Baldur's Gate)*, *(KOTOR)* is *Star Wars* done right.

Lucas Arts' *Star Wars: Knights of the Old Republic;*
a light saber fight.

Gamers may initially choose from a handful of character classes on which to base their persona, but the classes will branch, and new characters join your party that include Wookies (you know, the walking carpet), Twi'leks (the sexy dancers), and droids (the cute bleepie things). The combat is real time, but plausible, and based on a variation of the same rule set Bioware used in their heralded *Baldur's Gate* series.

The quests are awesome, spanning several planets, the graphics are state of the art, and the voice acting is some of the best that I have ever heard. The game has been out for over a year, but is still one of the hottest games on the Xbox. You can pick up a cheap copy on eBay or buy direct from Lucas Arts, Gamestop (http://www.gamestop.com), or most other Internet PC gaming retailers. You can't beat that with a light saber. If you like RPGs and *Star Wars*, you'll love *Knights of the Old Republic*.

Halo

Genre: Action
Publisher: Microsoft (www.microsoft.com)

This is the game that well and truly put the Xbox on the map, and is still the console's biggest seller. Everything about the game exudes perfectionistic quality. You play *Halo* as Master Chief (essentially a Space Navy SEAL). The game happens in a space-faring future, where Earth is fighting an alien race known as The Covenant. In the beginning of the game, you're awakened from cryo-sleep and learn that The Covenant is trying to obtain a mysterious artifact—perhaps a weapon—on an artificial ring-shaped world known as Halo, and it's up to you to prevent that from happening.

Microsoft's *Halo:* looks like a nice place to live, doesn't it?

X xbox

92

Yes, the game is a first-person shooter, but it is also so much more. Both the enemies and your allies (Earth Marines) display an artificial intelligence that is almost sentient. If you jump into one of the many drivable vehicles, nearby Marines will hop onboard and man the guns. Enemies will pin you with intense fire while another group attempts to outflank your position, and the bad guys will even send point men to seek you out.

And good looking? The visuals have to be seen to be believed. Some of the levels are majestic, and the firefights are better than San Francisco Bay on the Fourth of July. Multiplayer is a hoot to boot, and the story is better than much of what you buy in Barnes & Noble. Simply put, this is the best Xbox game available, and one of the best shooters anywhere, for any platform.

Madden NFL 2005

Genre: Sports
Publisher: EA Sports (www.ea.com)

The Electronic Arts "John Madden" branded football franchise has long been the dominant football franchise in the video game market. The 2005 version (released in August of 2004), further enhances the game's position and brings what may be the best console football game of all time to the Xbox.

The game has everything, and when I say everything, I mean *everything*. The kitchen sink is probably in there somewhere too, but I just haven't found it. *Madden NFL 2005* lets gamers control their men with the game pad, or run the game like they were the coach—selecting the play and then watching the result. The game has full seasons, franchise mode, or stuff as short as training drills to get you into the game.

The tough Ravens defense in
EA Sports *Madden NFL 2005*

Madden's 2005 edition places a bit more emphasis on defense than those in past years did. New to this game is the "hit stick" that allows defensive players to really unload on a nearby ball carrier. You may now also assign corner-backs to cover specific wide outs at the line of scrimmage, and even rearrange linebacker's zones. The offensive game is little changed from the previous year, but that isn't a bad thing; it was great last year.

In fact, *great* describes this whole game. If you are looking for one of the best football games of all time, you need look no further than *Madden NFL 2005*.

New and upcoming

The previously mentioned games are timeless. Although some of them are 2-3 years old, they are as good today as the day they were released. Nevertheless, we thought you might like a look at what's brand new and what's coming up in the near future. Some of these games, such as *Halo 2*, will be out in late 2004, others will be 2005, but whatever the release date, these are the upcoming Xbox games that I feel are worth waiting for.

Fable

> Genre: Role Playing
> Publisher: Microsoft (www.microsoft.com)

Designed by legendary designer, Peter Molyneux *(Black & White), Fable* is an epic role-playing game that takes gamers through the life (from birth to death) of a single character. As has become the rage as of late, the choices that players make will morph their game character into a good or bad person.

You begin as a child, running errands for your father and the local townsfolk. Even in these errands you may choose to do good or do bad.

Microsoft's *Fable*: don't worry, the tattoos are henna

Preface

Up and Running

Maximizing Your Xbox Experience

Networking the Xbox

Take it Online with Xbox Live

Xbox Accessories

Xbox Buyer's Guide

The Future Is Bright

X xbox

94

As you grow, you affiliate with either the peace-loving traders and become good, or with the treacherous bandits and become evil. In the extreme, your choices will affect how the character looks. An evil character's skin pales and he or she may even grow horns; good folks look healthy and happy.

Fable is an action-RPG. In other words, the combat is real time. You may choose to develop your character as an expert in melee, ranged combat, or magic. Even these paths will develop your character's appearance. Melee experts will grow strong, big, and somewhat slow. Archers will be lean, mean, and agile, whereas those well versed in magic will age more rapidly, and grow long white hair.

The game is fascinating, and like all Peter Molyneux titles, a unique experience. It promises to be one of the best role-playing games available for the Xbox.

Brothers in Arms

Genre: Action
Publisher: Ubisoft (www.ubisoft.com)

This title is put together by Gearbox—the same development studio that constructed Halo for PC. *Brothers in Arms* combines the best elements of action and strategy. Published by Ubisoft, *Brothers in Arms* follows the exploits of a squad of the 502nd Parachute Infantry Regiment as they fight their way through the fields, hedgerows, and towns of Normandy, France in June of 1944. The game provides the opportunity to wax German soldiers from a first-person view as well as control the squad in a manner similar to *Full Spectrum Warrior*.

Ubisoft's *Brothers in Arms* . . . look at those bullets fly by!

Preface

Up and Running

Maximizing Your Xbox Experience

Networking the Xbox

Take it Online with Xbox Live

Xbox Accessories

Xbox Buyer's Guide

The Future Is Bright

✕ XBOX

96

You play as Sergeant Matt Baker; initially you are alone, and the game differs little from *Call of Duty* or *Medal of Honor*, but as you find your squadmates, the game morphs into something new. In a typical mission, Baker controls himself and the squad's suppression and maneuver fire teams, each consisting of three men. The men in the fire teams are not ordered individually, but rather as a team, with Baker providing direction to the team leader, and the team members following the team leader's orders. For example, Baker might order the suppression team to pin a group of German soldiers in the house just up the road while both he and the assault team maneuver to the enemy flank, close in, and administer the coup de grace.

Gamers will be rewarded for not only possessing a quick trigger finger, but for also a quick mind. As in THQ's *Full Spectrum Warrior*, you'll need to use realistic squad tactics to defeat the enemy. The game is tense, the game is fun, and the game is challenging. Due out in early 2005, it looks to be a must-have for strategy and action fans alike.

Halo 2

Genre: Action
Publisher: Microsoft (www.microsoft.com)

Oh yeah, you know it, buddy. Like Microsoft's advertisement for the games says: "On November 9th, Earth will never be the same." *Halo 2* Is the most heavily hyped game in the history of Xboxdom, it will also probably be the biggest seller. Installment one finished with the destruction of the Halo world, and that—in a sense—is where *Halo 2* picks up. But this time the Covenant is playing for keeps—they are invading planet Earth.

Bungie has been very tight lipped about the game and the plot behind it, showing only one level at the Electronic Entertainment Exposition in 2003, but you may be sure that more of the high-caliber stuff will be jammed on this disk. The graphics are simply stunning. Bright laser bolts whip the air, explosions ripple, and Marines animate as if they were real. You'll still be able to pilot most anything that moves, and you'll also be able to blast the bad guys with a pistol in each hand—something that you couldn't do in the original game.

Microsoft's *Halo 2:* wow, good thing I remembered my power armor!

Preface

Up and
Running

Maximizing
Your Xbox
Experience

Networking
the Xbox

Take it
Online with
Xbox Live

Xbox
Accessories

Xbox
Buyer's Guide

The Future
Is Bright

✕ xʙox

98

Most of the same enemies return for a second round. You'll see Grunts, Jackals, and Elites, but you'll also get your first glimpse of the Prophets (the brains behind the operation), and the melee experts—the Brutes.

Multiplayer is as robust as before, and this time with Xbox Live already up and running (Xbox Live was not available when *Halo* originally shipped). There will be capture the flag, death match, and just about any way you want to play—LAN, online, split screen—*Halo 2* will accommodate you. *Halo* is hands down the greatest game ever made for the Xbox. Bungie is hoping the sequel will change all that.

MechAssault 2: Lone Wolf

Genre: BattleTech Simulation
Publisher: Microsoft (www.microsoft.com)

FASA's BattleTech is one of the most revered universes in science fiction. Originally conceived by Jordan Weisman (now CEO of Whiz Kids), the universe is as rich in story-telling depth as it is in action. Often copied, no one has ever quite achieved the mystique of FASA's giant, battling bipedal weapons platforms.

Microsoft's *Mech Assault 2*

The original *MechAssault* was an awesome game and much revered by BattleTech enthusiasts throughout gameland. Despite its age, it continues to be the most popular game on Xbox Live, and the second edition is sure to strengthen that position.

The main strengthening comes from the diversification of units. The original game was "Mech heavy" to say the least. In *Lone Wolf* players will not only have a plethora of 'Mechs, but also tanks, vertical take-off and landing (VTOL) aircraft, gun turrets, and a sultry woman in leather pants and a red shirt. You may now jack enemy 'Mechs by jumping on their backs, but to do so you will have to exit whatever you are riding, exposing yourself to enemy fire.

What gets overlooked in the multiplayer hype is the single player campaign. *MechAssault's* was good, and *Lone Wolf's* should be more of the same. Look for the game in early 2005.

And that's not all folks

As I said earlier, it would take another book to address the hundreds of available Xbox games. Game developers are supporting the console in a big way. Also coming out in the near future are *Knights of the Old Republic: The Sith Lords,* Id's epic shooter—*Doom 3*, EA's super soccer game—*FIFA 2005,* and a host of others. It's a great time to be an Xbox gamer, so turn on that console and dive right in.

Preface

Up and Running

Maximizing Your Xbox Experience

Networking the Xbox

Take it Online with Xbox Live

Xbox Accessories

Xbox Buyer's Guide

The Future Is Bright

07

The Future Is Bright

One of the best things about the Xbox is that despite the hundreds of available games, tens of accessories, and the thousands of gamers that want to meet you online, the whole Xbox thing is just beginning. The Xbox won't be Microsoft's only console, but rather their *first* console. In fact, the rumor mill indicates that Bill Gates may announce the Xbox-2 at the Consumer Electronic Show at Las Vegas in January of 2005. Now, you must understand that its takes some time from the announcement to having it sit in your entertainment stand, but still the future may be closer than you think. Ken Kutaragi, who is the CEO of Sony Computer Entertainment announced that Sony intends to have a playable version of the PlayStation 3 at the Electronic Entertainment Exposition of 2005 (May). You can be sure that Microsoft will *not* want to let Sony get too much of a lead on them in these console wars, so the Xbox-2 can't be far behind.

Preface

Up and Running

Maximizing Your Xbox Experience

Networking the Xbox

Take it Online with Xbox Live

Xbox Accessories

Xbox Buyer's Guide

The Future Is Bright

The Xbox-2 has been the subject of much speculation. What type of processor will it have, what type of games will it play, will it be part computer/part console? Indeed, the Xbox-2 is just a name of convenience. Microsoft has not yet named their newest creation, but no doubt Bill Gates will provide that information when he officially launches the next generation box. That said, I thought that you would still like to know what I have found out so far and see my best guesses on some of the most commonly asked questions

Console Wars

So who will win the console wars? That question has drawn much ink since the advent of second generation consoles. Is it Nintendo with their record for high-quality games such as *Metroid Prime 2*, Sony with their massive number of consoles sold planet-wide, or the technologically superior Xbox? Pundits have pontificated on widely disparate views of the console future from the demise of Nintendo to the Xbox's withdrawal from the race. Now it appears that none of that will be the case. All three companies are doing well, and if there will be an ultimate winner, there is no sign of it yet. In fact the only clear cut winner I see is you. That's right, this competition means that games are getting better, the console prices are kept down and the real winner of the console wars becomes gamers and their hard-earned dollars.

Your next box

Microsoft has strong ties with the computer industry. Talented hackers have already turned the Xbox into a perfectly capable, hard-working desktop computer (Although why anyone would want to take something as fun as the Xbox and turn it into a workhorse is beyond me). The thing has a hard drive in it. These facts have led to quite a bit of conjecture that usually goes like this, "Will I be able to upgrade my Xbox?" Well, ask no more my gaming friend, I have the definitive answer for you . . . maybe.

Of course you can upgrade your Xbox in all the ways that I mentioned previously—from DVD to wireless adapters, there is quite a bit that you can do to upgrade your Xbox. But I know that's not what you meant, and the answer to your real question is no . . . well sort of. Okay, I apologize for cracking smart, but it doesn't look as it Microsoft is going to release software or hardware add-ons that will upgrade the console's performance. It's probably too late in the product cycle to do that. What you have in your entertainment center is probably what you'll have when Microsoft releases their next generation Xbox. Manufacturers, including Microsoft, will continue to develop better accessories to be sure, but the core Xbox will not change, at least not without hacking it. And that is the "well, sort of" part of the answer.

> You can however, download new levels, characters, and skins via Xbox Live. Given that capability, it is certainly possible that Microsoft will also provide basic software upgrades through the service.

✕ xbox

The hackable option

As I've said earlier, this isn't a book about hacking the Xbox, but as you may also remember that the question of the day—or at least of this section—is can you upgrade the Xbox, and the answer is no. But if you are willing to pop the cover, get your hands dirty, and solder a couple of wires, you certainly can change the Xbox's capabilities. The similarities between Xbox and a computer have lead to a league of hackers who have done everything from morph the box into a desktop PC to merely changing the DVDs it will accept. If this is your bag, I suggest checking out XBox-Hacker (www.xbox-hacker.com) or Xboxhacker (www.xboxhacker.com).

www.xbox-hacker.com has a ton of Xbox hacking information

Your Xbox doesn't run Age of Empires II yet ...

Again the similarity between Xbox and PC rears its silicon head. Of course there are some rumors to fuel this fire. According to the CNNMoney web site, Peter Moore, corporate vice president of worldwide marketing and publishing for Microsoft's home and entertainment division says, "We would be remiss if we didn't look at consumer scenarios that take advantage of our strengths." The same article, published on May 27, 2004, states that a California research group named the B/S/R Group is conducting research on a "videogame system with a hard drive and a built-in fully functional PC."

That's enough to make me clean the wax out of my ears. Moore continued, "There will come a day . . . that PC games will be interchangeable between Windows and the Xbox." Of course the real question is what does Moore mean by "come a day"? Certainly not with the introduction of the next-generation Xbox. Microsoft has been telling their stable of developers to prepare for a launch for Xbox-2 in 2005. Seems like we should have heard something about that before now, doesn't it? Probably not. Although Microsoft is not denying that date, they don't want to play it up just yet. The Xbox is gaining quite a bit of momentum, and Microsoft doesn't want to spoil that momentum with talk of the next console just yet. But more later on the release date.

Will this be the next Xbox?

X xbox

Backward compatibility

Backward compatibility means that first-generation Xbox games will be playable on second-generation machines. The PlayStation 2 has it. All PlayStation games (that we know of) will play just fine on the PlayStation 2—in fact, most PS1 games look better on the PS2—Microsoft has been tight-lipped on the backward compatibility issue.

Because Microsoft won't say, it's hard to know for sure, but the signs don't look good for backward compatibility. It appears that Microsoft will not use Intel to design the processor for the Xbox-2, nor will they employ NVidia to make the GPU. All indications are that the next generation Xbox will use an ATI video processing unit (VPU). Microsoft will also partner with IBM to produce the Xbox-2's processor. This means that the Xbox-2 will have a fundamentally different core processing unit than the Xbox, and the likelihood of it being backward compatible appear slim. However, vague rumors have surfaced indicating that some of the Microsoft Virtual PC team's responsibilities have been delegated to the Xbox team. And what does Virtual PC do but emulate a stock Pentium CPU on an IBM chip? Could that be the seed of backward-compatibility for the Xbox-2? Only time will tell...

PlayStation games, like *Vagrant Story*
(pictured right), play just fine on the
PlayStation 2

What are the specs?

No one knows what the specifications will be. There are, however, some educated guesses based on the information that Microsoft has already released. They look like this:

- Processor: Should be above 3GHz, and that's fast by anyone's standards. It won't be based on the Intel x86 standards, but rather on new IBM technology.

- Graphics: An ATI VPU—a unique term recently coined by ATI for the GPU that is the proverbial "rose by any other name"—will handle the game's visuals. www.thenextbox.com speculates that it may be based on the ATI R500 chip. Looks like we are talking 256MB of shared system RAM, 10MB of RAM dedicated to the VPU, and support for HDTV resolutions up to 1920 x 1080. (Shared system RAM means that the processor and VPU will share the RAM; the system and/or the game will determine the balance of working memory (system RAM) and the RAM used for 3D graphics.)

- The latest Dolby sound.

- A large—some sources say 80GB—internal/removable hard drive. That means you'll be able to pull the hard drive out of your box, slam it into your friend's, and play all your saved games over there. Sounds sweet.

- Four controller ports, perhaps two USB ports, an Ethernet port, and maybe a Firewire port. That's some serious portage.

Will the next-generation Xbox have a Firewire port like this?

Preface

Up and
Running

Maximizing
Your Xbox
Experience

Networking
the Xbox

Take it
Online with
Xbox Live

Xbox
Accessories

Xbox
Buyer's Guide

The Future
Is Bright

X xbox

When will the console hit the shelves? My best guess is 2006. I base that guess on several pieces of evidence. The largest is game development time. It takes 18 months (at a minimum) to develop a quality—triple A, as they say—title. This is the type of title that you want when you release a console. To release in 2005, even late 2005, that would mean that Microsoft has had developers working on next-generation games for at least four to six months. Although several companies, such as Activision, have acknowledged that they are working on next-generation software, several key developers, such as Bungie (the *Halo* series), and Bioware (*Knights of the Old Republic*), are either just wrapping up or neck-deep in projects for the current Xbox, such as *Halo 2* (Bungie) and *Jade Empire* (Bioware). Certainly they aren't developing software for a next-generation Xbox as of September 2004.

Steve Ballmer, the Microsoft CEO, has stated that there won't be a new Xbox in fiscal year 2005, which ends in mid-summer. So if Xbox is going to come out in 2005, it will be fall or winter 2005. Again, that looks like too little time to get the quality titles ready needed to ensure a successful launch.

Although Microsoft has vowed not to give Sony a head start this time (the PlayStation 2 released 18 months before the Xbox), it looks like the earliest the PS3 will release in Japan is spring of 2006. Given that, it seems likely that Microsoft will shoot for a summer 2006 release in the United States. Sorry folks, but it looks like we'll just have to wait. But I know it will be worth it.

Index

Preface

Up and
Running

Maximizing
Your Xbox
Experience

Networking
the Xbox

Take it
Online with
Xbox Live

Xbox
Accessories

Xbox
Buyer's Guide

The Future
Is Bright

X XBOX

Preface

Up and
Running

Maximizing
Your Xbox
Experience

Networking
the Xbox

Take it
Online with
Xbox Live

Xbox
Accessories

Xbox
Buyer's Guide

The Future
Is Bright

X XBOX